SEE, JUDGE, ACT

CATHOLIC SOCIAL TEACHING AND SERVICE LEARNING

REVISED EDITION

ERIN M. BRIGHAM

ANSELM
ACADEMIC

Created by the publishing team of Anselm Academic.

Cover images: shutterstock.com

Printed in the United States of America

7084

ISBN 978-1-59982-943-2

Author Acknowledgments

Many talented and generous people contributed to this book. On the top of the list, I would like to thank Maura Hagarty, editorial director at Anselm Academic, whose patient and insightful guidance made this book possible. I am incredibly grateful to Jennifer Reed-Bouley for her careful review of the book. Jennifer's dedication to her students and her passion for Catholic social teaching contributed a number of improvements to this text.

I would also like to thank supportive and inspiring colleagues at the University of San Francisco (USF), particularly Mike Duffy, former director of the Joan and Ralph Lane Center for Catholic Studies and Social Thought, as well as Lo Schiavo Chair, William O'Neill, and prior Lo Schiavo Chair, Thomas Massaro. I have been blessed with exceptional department chairs who have supported my professional development and mentored me in my teaching and writing, especially Lois Lorentzen and Vincent Pizzuto. I am most grateful for the many USF faculty who motivated me in the Thursday writing group over the past couple of years.

Like many faculty members, I started teaching a service-learning course with great intentions but with little knowledge about how to make service learning successful. I have been fortunate to learn from dedicated community partners, especially the Faithful Fools Street Ministry. I have also relied on the resources of USF's Leo T. McCarthy Center for Public Service and the Common Good. David Donahue, Julie Reed, Star Moore, Andrea Wise, and the student Advocates for Community Engagement have influenced my approach to service learning and have helped me work through a number of service-learning dilemmas over the years.

I would also like to thank my students of Catholic social thought, who have taught me the most about the value of service learning. I have watched students begin the class with a fear of leaving campus and finish the semester with a real appreciation for one of the overlooked communities in San Francisco—communities that tourists often miss but that bring so much life to this great city. It is truly a privilege to witness the transformative potential of education.

Finally, I want to thank my husband, Dana Wolfe. Every challenge is easier and every accomplishment is sweeter since I found a great partner.

Publisher Acknowledgments

Thank you to Jennifer Reed-Bouley of the College of Saint Mary, Omaha, Nebraska, for reviewing this work in progress.

In this revised edition of *See, Judge, Act*, Erin Brigham skillfully updates her substantive yet accessible introduction to Catholic social teaching and praxis. Incorporating newly relevant signs of the times and insights from Pope Francis, this edition offers a preface with valuable pedagogical guidance for those forming students for social change. Together with her community partner, Brigham offers insights into how service learning pedagogy can disrupt standard assumptions and help participants to understand their own well-being as bound up with the flourishing of those whom they encounter. I will continue to use this book in my undergraduate classroom and highly recommend it for others.

—Kristin E. Heyer, Boston College

We will never be able to respond to social crises effectively and ethically unless we study issues of social justice. The first step is to learn how to learn, and this volume provides the key. Erin Brigham taps her impressive experience in service learning to share the methodology of social analysis, along with wise and original insights into complex and disputed issues of social justice. Including the crises of immigration and the environment, the book is even more relevant and urgent than it was when the original edition appeared just a few years ago. This is that rare book that successfully bridges the world of academic theology and hands-on experience. Rooted in the tradition of Catholic social teaching and committed to a pedagogy of engaged learning, this timely and user-friendly volume is a uniquely valuable resource for our time.

—Thomas Massaro, SJ, Fordham University

Professor Erin M. Brigham's book critically explores the intersections of theology, service learning, and the Catholic social tradition for our contemporary context. Her commitment to helping faculty and the next generation learn about both the richness of those intersections and the challenges they present is robust and compelling. Theoretically grounded, empirically invigorating and pedagogically engaging, this book provides faculty a great resource and invites students to a disciplined understanding of what it means to see, judge, and act in a world of great injustices. A debt of gratitude is owed Brigham for the quality of her research and writing, the depth of her community collaboration, and the clarity of her pedagogical awareness that are so clearly evident in this searching and graceful book.

—Kathleen Maas Weigert, Loyola University Chicago

The new edition of *See, Judge, Act* is a splendid introduction to the rich heritage of modern Catholic social teaching. Even more, in the spirit of Pope Francis's pastoral theology, it offers an invaluable guide to *living* the tradition in the context of service learning. Here teaching and learning go hand in hand: following the hermeneutical logic of the pastoral circle or spiral in responding to the "signs of the times," Prof. Brigham brings the wisdom of a vital tradition to bear on such critical issues as poverty, migration, workers' rights, white privilege and racial and ethnic bias, solidarity in peacemaking, and the global ecological crisis. Deserving a wide readership, especially in these contentious times, Brigham's new *See, Judge, Act* gives us reason to hope that the Church's social teaching will cease to be our "best-kept secret."

—William O'Neill, Jesuit School of Theology of Santa Clara University

Contents

Foreword

Paul J. Fitzgerald, SJ, President, University of San Francisco

Undergraduate students at a Catholic university can either learn about theology or they can learn to theologize. The former is a valuable endeavor of appropriation of the thought of many great minds that have carried a tradition forward. The latter is the inescapable obligation of a person whose own faith has come alive.

One quite promising way to awaken a "faith that does justice" is to be found in this book. Students will indeed learn about a coherent body of teaching collectively referred to as Catholic social thought. By doing so in the context of a service-learning course, students are invited and empowered to appropriate the undergirding insights of that tradition, its inner dynamism, in such a way as to become practitioners, theologians, themselves. Alternating, as this book does, between the classroom and the social service agency affords students the possibility to become participant observers and partners in sustained dialogues that support a common exploration of the social obligations that arise from faith.

Theologizing in the context of the urban poor requires that students be willing to discover and consider carefully their own biases and be willing to bracket them as they seek to see social reality through new frames, from new vantage points. As St. Anselm continues to remind us, theology is faith seeking understanding, and ever more so, we know that this search takes place in complex social contexts. Student participation in communities of the urban poor is both limiting and freeing at the same time. Students quickly come to understand that a person's point of view is always partial, always biased, for there is no Archimedean point, no vantage outside of social reality to afford us an objective view of ourselves and our world. We can only view reality from within a life-world, and we can only hope to make our view more generous, and critique our biases, if and as we move thoughtfully, respectfully, and with an open mind into other life-worlds. Perhaps we can venture no further than the border areas of these new-to-us life-worlds. Modesty and candor impose on us the admission that we cannot be fully at home in multiple cultural worlds, but we can at least be a respectful guest in the life-world of the urban poor. Through engaging multiple perspectives, and especially the perspective of the poor, we can gain a more catholic view, a more nuanced and complex view, and thereby a greater understanding of a truth beyond ourselves, a truth that attracts and impels us, a truth that grasps us fully even as we only grasp at it.

To do theology in the context of marginalized communities liberates us, changing our concerns and suggesting new avenues of exploration. When we purposefully read scripture from the point of view of the homeless family we have come to know through a service-learning placement, new levels of meaning appear in the text. Teachers in this learning context must be willing guides to their students, helping them to surface and set aside previously learned theories, assumptions, and premises that are no longer adequate to the task of theologizing in this new context. This can be jarring to students. They can experience this shattering of their prior conceptual framework as a crisis. Yet it is in moments of crisis that we are free to construct a new synthesis of theory and practice. This allows us to see far more clearly the reality in front of us, judge in a far more nuanced way what we must do, and act far more intentionally in that undertaking.

Preface to Revised Edition
Letter to Educators

Erin Brigham, University of San Francisco
Sam Dennison, Faithful Fools Street Ministry

Discussions about service learning tend to focus solely on what students are supposed to learn and how. The experience for all involved, however, becomes richer when faculty, students, and community members—each with a unique perspective—form a learning community. Since 2014, we, Erin Brigham and Sam Dennison, have been partners in offering the course "Women, Poverty, and Catholic Social Thought." Both of us have facilitated service learning in a variety of formats. Some formats have been more successful than others. In this letter to educators, we highlight some things we have learned about crafting service-learning experiences.

The Partnership and the Course

Erin Brigham and Sam Dennison

The course "Women, Poverty, and Catholic Social Thought" examines gender and intersectional identities in the context of poverty and other social inequalities. Working alongside Faithful Fools Street Ministry, students meet daily for three weeks in the Tenderloin—a condensed and densely populated San Francisco neighborhood. Faithful Fools is a small, nonprofit organization: two full-time staff, a few full-time and many part-time volunteers. The staff live and work in an economically impoverished neighborhood in a very wealthy city. Their mission statement calls them to be present and meet people where they are. The specifics of what the Fools provide—art programs, advocacy, direct service, and so on—varies depending upon who shows up—outside volunteers or neighbors in the Tenderloin or both. With education being a primary focus of the Fools, a key offering is the Street Retreat, in which participants are invited to spend a day walking through the neighborhood of the Tenderloin with intentionality, reflecting on oneself and one's relationship to the surrounding community.

Faithful Fools and Street Retreats

Sam Dennison

Faithful Fools Street Ministry is a live/work nonprofit in the Tenderloin neighborhood of San Francisco. Everything the ministry does is about growing relationships and community. From poetry writing to community advocacy, each action is a time to build respect and trust. The ministry welcomes everyone and focuses on each person's talents and worth.

Street Retreats are the founding act of Faithful Fools. From the very beginning, this practice has helped people reflect upon the assumptions, fears, and experiences that influence their day-in and day-out interactions in the Tenderloin. Faithful Fools began doing Street Retreats in June 1998. Since then nearly 6,000 people (ranging in age from 13 to 83) have spent all or part of a day engaged with the Tenderloin, not as the object of a guided tour, but as a retreat center. This practice has enabled people to form relationships and recognize their common humanity. It has also built a foundation for shared learning and practice. The streets level people. We all make contact with the sidewalk, if only for a moment as we leave our front doors; we are all on the same plane, none higher, none lower than another. Not only is the Street Retreat Faithful Fools' founding act, it is at the center of the Fools' ministry. Faithful Fools' mission statement says "we discover on the streets our common humanity." Learn more about the Faithful Fools Street Ministry at *www.faithfulfools.org*.

The course engages students in reading and discussion of texts on theories of justice and intersectionality along with Catholic theology and Catholic social teaching. Those ideas become contextualized through activities and conversations with residents of the neighborhood. A primary pedagogical tool is the students' ongoing reflection on their experience in the community and within themselves as they walk the streets for a period of time each day. As their final project, students are invited to create a booklet in which they summarize, synthesize, and collaboratively arrange quotes from reflection papers and texts, original works of art, poetry, and narrative.

Promising Practices—A Faculty Perspective

Erin Brigham

Strong partnerships are key to successful service learning. My relationship to the Faithful Fools began with my own street retreat and has evolved over years of contact, commitment, and collaboration. Participating in the activities of the community partner, developing a deeper understanding of the context of learning, and maintaining regular communication are key to developing strong partnerships. The first time I taught the course, I designed the syllabus on my own and missed the opportunity to harness the wisdom and resources of the community partner to engage students. By the third time, the topics, immersion experiences, and assignments emerged out of a shared syllabus and multiple conversations with the community partner.

As a result, diverse activities were integrated into the course that augmented the academic content and contributed to multiple dimensions of student learning. These included an experience with Theater of the Oppressed[1] that prepared students to attend a public hearing involving a dispute between a group of Catholic nuns running a dining hall for low-income families and members of an adjacent homeowner's association. Students also had the opportunity to meet community organizers working for empowerment with residents of the Tenderloin seeking to exercise their right to vote. A number of students identified these experiences as key learning moments in the course.

---

1. Influenced by educator Paulo Freire and developed by Brazilian theater director Augusto Boal, this form of theater is designed to promote social change. Audience members are active participants, using their bodies to represent social realities, conflicts, feelings, and experiences. Forms of Theater of the Oppressed are used throughout the world to promote problem-solving, conflict resolution, community organizing, and activism.

Service learning invites collaboration and flexibility. Working with the Fools has disabused me of the perception that I can or should control the learning in the class. Faculty are challenged with the task of discerning when to be flexible with the content of the course and when to redirect the readings, conversation, and experiences toward the learning outcomes of the syllabus. Thinking back on the first time I taught the course, I found myself trying to create a traditional classroom experience on-site with the community partner. What I realized over time is that community engagement offers unforeseen opportunities for learning and sometimes this requires detours from the syllabus.

For example, as a result of the service-learning experiences, the course on women and poverty involved more reading and discussion around race than I had anticipated when creating the course. Students watched the documentary *13th* and participated in a workshop on harm reduction,[2] which generated interest among the students to go deeper into the reality of racism. Rather than detracting from the learning outcomes, this deepened engagement around theories of justice, intersectionality, and Catholic social thought.

In a service-learning course, everyone teaches and learns together through reflection. In a service-learning course in particular, the curriculum goes beyond the expertise of faculty. Learning that involves self-examination with respect to one's assumptions, beliefs, and values in relationship to observations in the community breaks down the roles of teacher and learner. Effective reflection makes concrete connections between the academic content and students' experiences in the community.

Just as students must be challenged to reflect on the systemic and structural dimensions of the issues they encounter as well as their biases and stereotypes that are surfaced, faculty members are also challenged to continually examine their relationship to the community. I have integrated the practice of keeping a teaching journal to reflect on my experiences during the course and my own growth in solidarity with the community. The course on women and poverty

---

2. Harm reduction offers strategies aimed at reducing negative consequences associated with certain behaviors such as drug use. A number of advocates of Harm Reduction see it as a way to promote the dignity and rights of people who use drugs while minimizing the harm to individuals and communities.

integrated reflection in a number of ways—classroom discussion and writing assignments on specific questions related to the reading and service. The final project of creating the booklet engaged student creativity and affectivity and challenged students to identify the most meaningful learning outcomes from the course.

Institutional support promotes sustainable and effective service learning. Proponents of service learning advocate for institutional commitment in the form of faculty training and incentives as well as the investment of university research and resources in the interest of community partners. At my university, the Leo T. McCarthy Center for Public Service and the Common Good employs leaders in the field of community engagement who train faculty and community partners in best practices and offer ongoing support for service-learning courses. The university also offers an Arrupe Justice Immersion program that provides a stipend for the community partner in recognition of the labor the partner invests in the course.

Successful service learning problematizes traditional models of service. If I have learned anything from working with the Faithful Fools, it is an approach to service that follows relationship. The course created opportunities for students to engage in diverse forms of service. They accompanied community members as participants in a recovery circle. They supported advocacy by participating in a community-organizing effort to empower residents to vote. And they supported meal services by setting up, serving, and cleaning up after meals. The final project highlighted the ways in which students benefitted from the service and grew in awareness of how their own flourishing is connected to the community members they met.

Promising Practices—A Community Partner Perspective

Sam Dennison

Imagine the possibilities beyond service hours. For Faithful Fools, identifying meaningful service learning is a little more difficult than it is for larger agencies like soup kitchens or after-school programs. We do not have standardized volunteer hours that need filling;

rather our programs are constantly changing as the needs around us change. So, at one point in time, we may be providing visual arts and poetry programs and at another helping resident activists to register and mobilize voters. While much of what we do illustrates different aspects of Catholic social thought, the needs of our neighborhood are not such that we can plan on having the same projects or volunteer slots every semester.

Because our needs vary, at times we struggle to meet the needs of service-learning classes. Without regular hours or a structured volunteer program, we are not always able to give students convenient schedules as easily as other service providers often do. But working with Erin and other faculty like her, we have found that we can be creative and look beyond service hours and create deeply satisfying learning experiences that benefit both us and students.

The first thing we do is set aside the idea that we are providing a certain number of hours for students to volunteer. Rather, we look for projects and tasks that compliment what students are doing in the class, and we focus on how we will spend our time together, not how much time is required. In practice, this means that we find ways to work together in small groups and sometimes even one-on-one. The time requirement is determined by the project's need and not the syllabus.

Whatever initiative we are working on, the underlying purpose is to have instructor and students eventually articulate their relationship to us and to our community. The process of reflection from the outset of each service-learning relationship, combined with working together, face-to-face, creates an academic *and* a visceral learning experience. For us, the process of reflection embedded in these relationships is an ongoing source of feedback, insight, and connection. Through this praxis model, built on cycles of action and reflection, we form a community that blends service and learning for all of us. We try to ensure that the task itself is valuable, to be sure, but key for us is the learning through relationship building. It is through relationship that we (students, faculty, and Fools alike) learn about and have an impact on the issues affecting our neighborhood.

Deepening engagement requires commitment and trust. When Erin and I began to work closely on designing this class, I found myself reading the principles of Catholic social thought with new insights, understanding for the first time that the visceral experiences of our neighborhood and the relationships with the people who live here could change how students think about social injustice as it intersects their own lives.

We focused the class on engaging in the community directly, not abstractly. We began to pair readings with community engagement so that discussions of "Solidarity" or "The Dignity of the Human Person" came alive through both readings and popular education workshops like Theater of the Oppressed.

We also integrated more art into the class because art and creativity are survival tools for many people living in poverty. If students were to understand the complexities of life in our neighborhood, they had to be able to synthesize what they were learning and what they were seeing around them, using the resources (especially making art) that members of the community use to make sense of what is happening to them. So, we had students create a booklet together, with each student contributing a page with words and images depicting what the student had learned. This structure of creative engagement made it possible for us to delve deeply into some difficult issues, including the US history of slavery, mass incarceration, and racism. It also gave students a chance to work directly with community artist-activists.

For all of us—Erin and the Faithful Fools—working together has changed our understanding of both service and learning. We became partners in a deeper sense as we learned to trust each other.

The most meaningful service provokes this question: *How is my well-being bound up with yours?* There is one more thing that has shaped how we Faithful Fools are approaching service learning as a result of these different collaborations. We have become insistent on working together and shaping assignments together well in advance of the first day of class. This is certainly true when we are doing intensive courses like "Women, Poverty, and Catholic Social Thought," but it is also true when we are working within the structure of a semester-long course with specific service-learning requirements, including hours.

What we learned from working with Erin is that a collaborative relationship matters more than anything else. Through collaboration we can take advantage of whatever flexibility is available in a given class. If it is a class with several community partners, and each student has essentially the same final project—thereby limiting flexibility, we can still shape student expectations and experience by working together early in the process. If there is greater latitude because there are fewer community partners or it is an intensive course, then we can shape assignments more or provide community resources to enhance the course. Whatever the constraints, it is the way that we collaborate that makes the service learning mutually beneficial.

Beyond the essential characteristic of collaboration, we have come to value the content of our work together as well. Over these years of collaboration, we have come to understand that the most meaningful service that students can do in a class on Catholic social thought is to address this question: *How is my well-being bound up with yours?*

This question guides just about everything that we do. It keeps us from distancing ourselves from complexities of the neighborhood or taking the humanity of the people around us for granted. We make sure we are all asking this question—students and community members alike. Sometimes people in our neighborhood dismiss students as privileged and naïve, not realizing how many are first-generation college students or that some have grown up in and out of homeless shelters. Some students come into the neighborhood and find themselves surprised at the number of working families living there or the degree of mutual care among people who are living on the streets. I remember one student's reflection as he worked out his response to this question: "I always thought that people were poor because they did something wrong. It never occurred to me that someone could end up homeless through no fault of their own. Even me or my family could end up homeless."

While his observation may seem on some level terribly naïve, it is also a first step in understanding that we live in a world not of our own making and we are subject to large, sometimes invisible forces. Without moments like this—seeing and understanding how assumptions about fault and blame distance us from the realities of poverty—it is so much harder to understand why we need both compassion and activism if we are seeking to live in a just society.

It is these surprises about how poverty happens and how people end up in places they never expected to (sometimes for better and sometimes for worse) that make us see the reality of "if it can happen to you, it can happen to me." And if that is so, then my well-being is deeply bound up with yours . . . and your well-being is bound up with mine.

It is always my hope that some version of this question—How is your well-being bound up with mine?—is part of every class. It turns the service into learning and, with a little luck and a little bit of time, it may well turn learning into a life of service. I do not imagine that every service-learning student will take on a life of service, but I do hope that most will carry this sense of connection with them into their careers in marketing or human relations or nursing or physics or engineering. And if they do, perhaps when they are voting or making decisions about who to hire or how to budget or what policies to put into practice, they will remember how their own well-being is bound up with the people around them—in the workplace, in their families, and on the streets.

Resources for Service Learning

Ash, S.L., Clayton, P.H., and Atkinson, M.P. "Integrating reflection and assessment to capture and improve student learning." *Michigan Journal of Community Service Learning*, vol. 11, no. 2 (2005): 49–60.

Astin, A.W., Vogelgesang, L.J., Ikeda, E.K., and Yee, J.A. *How Service Learning Affects Students.* Los Angeles: Higher Education Research Institute, University of California, Los Angeles, 2000.

Bringle, R. G., and Hatcher, J.A. "Reflection in Service Learning: Making Meaning of Experience." *Educational Horizons,* vol. 77, no. 4 (1999): 179–85.

Butin, Dan Wernaa. "The Limits of Service Learning in Higher Education." *The Review of Higher Education,* vol. 29, no. 4 (2006): 473–98.

Campus Compact. *https://compact.org/.*

Campus Compact. *Introduction to Service-Learning Toolkit: Readings and Resources for Faculty,* 2nd ed. Providence, RI: Campus Compact, 2003.

Furco, A. "Service-Learning: A Balanced Approach to Experiential Education." In Taylor, B., ed. *Expanding Boundaries: Serving and Learning*. Washington, DC: Corporation for National Service, 1996.

Hatcher, J.A., Bringle, R.G., and Muthiah, R. "Designing Effective Reflection: What Matters to Service-Learning?" *Michigan Journal of Community Service Learning*, vol. 11, no. 1 (2004): 38–46.

Mitchell, T. D. "Traditional vs. Critical Service-Learning: Engaging the Literature to Differentiate Two Models." *Michigan Journal of Community Service Learning*, vol. 14, no. 2 (2008): 50–65.

Stoecker, R., and Tryon, E., eds. *The Unheard Voices: Community Organizations and Service Learning*. Philadelphia: Temple University Press, 2009.

Introduction

The main title of this text repeats a phrase—*see-judge-act*—associated with Belgian Catholic priest Joseph Cardijn, who worked with lay Catholics to connect their faith with social action. During the post–World War I era, an era marked by economic depression, Cardijn reached out to young working-class Catholics by founding the Young Christian Workers (YCW) in 1924.[1] The organization provided a place for laypeople to relate their struggles for justice in the workplace to an emerging tradition of Catholic social thought.[2] Cardijn introduced the process of seeing, judging, and acting in meetings of the YCW to encourage people to observe situations, to evaluate them based on the Gospels, and to act in ways that respond to observed injustices.

The YCW was just one of a number of Catholic associations that mobilized laypeople to address social issues during this era. Others include the Catholic Worker movement founded by Dorothy Day and Peter Maurin and Friendship House established by Catherine De Hueck.[3] As the young people involved in the YCW moved on to new phases of life, new types of movements emerged. For example, in 1949, Pat and Patty Crowley founded the Christian Family Movement, which went beyond the earlier movements by encouraging Catholics and adherents of other religions to work together to bring about social justice for families.[4] Cardijn's use of the see-judge-act process with the YCW highlights an important aspect of the Catholic social tradition: everyone—lay and ordained—shares responsibility for social analysis and action.

---

1. Joseph Willke, "The Worker-Priest Experiment in France," *America* (April, 1984): 253.

2. Ibid.

3. See Marvin Mich, *Catholic Social Teaching and Movements* (New London, CT: Twenty-Third Publications, 1998), 62–72.

4. Ibid., 72.

21

Pope Francis connects action for justice with the call to holiness that belongs to every follower of Christ. One should not look solely to priests, bishops, nuns, and saints for models of holiness, Francis argues, but to the daily life of everyone building love, justice, and peace in the world.[5] Holiness, in his view, is not about withdrawing from the world or engaging in simple acts of charity. Rather, it involves seeking Christ among the poor and marginalized and working for the social conditions that honor their dignity.[6]

Though the phrase *see-judge-act* emerged in a Catholic context, it describes a process that people use implicitly and explicitly in many different contexts to observe situations, to evaluate them in light of understandings of what is good and right, and to act in ways to improve those situations. History is full of examples of inspiring people who model this process. Civil rights leader Martin Luther King Jr. observed the social injustices perpetuated by racism in the United States, drew on his faith and values to denounce racism as morally evil, and acted out of his convictions to advocate for racial justice. Nobel Peace Prize recipient Saint Mother Teresa saw the suffering caused by poverty on the streets of Calcutta, reflected on the situation in light of teachings of the Gospels, and responded with compassionate service. Jesuit priest Greg Boyle saw the impact of concentrated gang violence in Los Angeles and was personally transformed by encounters with former gang members. Driven by a faith-filled commitment to human dignity, Fr. Boyle started Homeboy Industries to empower former gang members to escape the cycle of violence and incarceration. Also, consider the college student who observes educational inequalities in her city, evaluates the situation based on her conviction that everyone should have the opportunity to receive a good education, and decides to tutor low-income youth on a regular basis.

This book provides an introduction to both the Catholic social tradition and the process of seeing, judging, and acting. It is designed especially for service-learning courses that invite students to *see* social situations, *judge* them in light of principles drawn from the Catholic

---

5. Pope Francis, *Gaudete et exsultate* (*On the Call to Holiness in Today's World*), 2018, no. 14.

6. Ibid., nos. 95–99.

Church's social teaching and from their own values and beliefs, and *act* in response to observed injustices. This introduction will provide an overview of the three steps or stages of the see-judge-act process, discuss the use of the process in conjunction with service learning, and explore the relationship between the process and the Catholic social tradition.

The See-Judge-Act Process

See: Social Analysis

Seeing, or social analysis, goes beyond first impressions, which tend to yield incomplete pictures. An observer's first impressions are often influenced by his or her expectations and assumptions and based on limited information. Consider for example two US college students on a study abroad trip to Manila. When the students see small children begging for money on the street, one points out the failure of the government to provide a safety net for vulnerable citizens and the other student cites the failure of parents to provide for their children. Both judgments uncover assumptions: one about the role of government, the other about the agency of individual families living in poverty.

Catholic social ethicists Peter Henriot and Joe Holland define social analysis as "the effort to obtain a more complete picture of a social situation by exploring its historical and structural relationships."[7] Whereas historical analysis considers how a situation developed and changed over time, structural analysis assesses how structures such as the economy, politics, and social and cultural norms relate to the situation. Social analysts also consider who makes decisions affecting people in the situation and the values underlying those decisions.

Henriot and Holland point out that social situations are complex and that the results of one's analysis are always limited.[8] Despite this limitation, social analysis can help people see a situation more accurately than they could based on impressions, and this analytical

---

7. Joe Holland and Peter Henriot, *Social Analysis: Linking Faith and Justice* (Maryknoll, NY: Orbis and Washington, DC: Center of Concern, 1983), 14.

8. Ibid., 15–16.

seeing can lead to more effective judgments and actions. In the previous example, it would be important for the students to understand the local and national policies and initiatives to address poverty as well as the historical and cultural impact of poverty on the community. Furthermore, social analysis would uncover the impact of colonization and dynamics of gender, race, and class within the family and society that influence the observed realities.

Judge: Ethical Reflection

The second step, judging, involves evaluating a situation in light of guiding principles that define what is good and right, which can be drawn from any number of sources—religious doctrine, scriptures, cultural mores, philosophical perspectives, the teachings of inspirational figures. The goal of this step is to formulate a response to a problematic social situation.

Individuals evaluate the data differently, in part, because of differences in their values, priorities, and visions of what is good and right. Judging involves selecting a set of principles to use as criteria for evaluation, but it also involves recognizing that no one approaches a reality as a blank slate and assessing one's own beliefs and values and how they shape one's judgments.

Reflection makes explicit the values, commitments, and beliefs that are constantly shaping how a person relates to the world. In doing so, it challenges people to be cognizant of how they judge what they see and also whether or not what they see in the world *and* how they act in the world conform to their deepest convictions. It might also lead to a transformation of one's convictions based on new experiences and information.

Returning to the students in Manila, it is worth considering the experiences, assumptions, and values that might have influenced their initial judgment. As college students from the United States, each of them enjoys considerable economic and political privilege. Encountering people who lack such privilege, coupled with social analysis and reflection, could prompt the students to evaluate their beliefs and values about the situation. Perhaps the student who applied the value of family responsibility to the situation comes to see how oppression due to class, race, and gender limits one's ability to protect and provide for one's family. This shift in perspective might prompt her to consider how other principles—solidarity and participation—might lead her to a more effective response.

Act: Charity and Justice

Seeing and judging lead to step three—acting. The concepts of charity and justice help distinguish types of action. Charity responds to people's immediate needs, often for food, shelter, safety, and clothing. It tends to flow from a spirit of altruism and generosity or a feeling of compassion for other people. Justice aims to address the reasons why people are without adequate resources and usually requires long-term collaborative efforts with community members. This is because acting to bring about justice can involve changing systems, policies, and institutions. People who work for justice are often motivated by a sense of obligation to a vision of goodness, justice, and fairness. Charity and justice are not isolated actions and so one's response to a particular situation may involve both. However, distinguishing between charity and justice can be a helpful reminder that each aim is important and incomplete without the other. When charity is seen as a starting point for fostering solidarity, it can be an effective way to promote empathy across social divisions and respond to people's immediate needs. However, charity without justice can ignore the structural inequalities that set up the need for charity in the first place and even reinforce unjust relationships. Later chapters will elaborate more thoroughly on these important concepts.[9]

Service, Learning, and the See-Judge-Act Process

Many people associate the term *service* primarily with charitable acts aimed at meeting immediate needs such as providing meals, clothing, or shelter to people living in poverty. These actions are sometimes referred to as direct service; however, the term *service* in service learning also encompasses actions aimed at bringing about justice. One

---

9. See also Tom Massaro, *Living Justice: Catholic Social Teaching in Action*. Second Classroom Edition (Lanham, MD: Rowman and Littlefield, 2012), chapter 1.

type of justice-oriented service is advocacy, using one's voice to speak on behalf of someone who lacks social, political, and economic influence. For example, someone might serve hotel workers trying to form a union by writing letters to the hotel management in support of the workers' struggle. Justice-oriented service can involve empowering individuals and communities to create structural changes. Service as empowerment might involve educating domestic workers about their rights so they can take legal action if they have experienced exploitation in the form of wage theft or sexual harassment. Take a moment to consider your understanding of the term *service*. How does your understanding relate to direct service, advocacy, and empowerment? How have experiences of providing or receiving various forms of service influenced your perspective?

Preparing for a Service-Learning Course

Particularly in the United States, a context that tends to value and reward volunteerism, service is understood in this framework.[10] Service learning and volunteering, however, are not the same. The distinction is important because each approach promotes a different way of relating to the community. Successful service learning is characterized by reciprocity. In other words, all stakeholders in the relationship (students, educators, and community partners) should benefit from and have a voice in the relationship.

One of the challenges to achieving reciprocity in a service-learning context mirrors the challenge of achieving reciprocity in society—people have unequal access to power, influence, and resources. Such inequalities are often a result of unearned privilege—assets and power that one experiences by belonging to a particular social group. Consider how a woman might avoid walking alone after

---

10. Because people commonly associate service with charity and volunteerism some educators prefer the language of community engagement to service. This critique is well developed in Randy Stoecker, *Liberating Service Learning and the Rest of Higher Education Civic Engagement* (Philadelphia: Temple University Press, 2016). I have chosen to retain the language of service learning while rejecting simplistic notions of service, taking instead a more expansive view that includes advocacy, empowerment, and community organizing for social change. For a more detailed discussion of types of service that include advocacy and justice education see Marvin Mich, *Catholic Social Teaching and Movements* (New London, CT: Twenty-Third Publications, 1998).

Spectrum of Activities Related to Service Learning

Andrew Furco locates service learning on a spectrum of activities related to service and experiential education. Unlike volunteering, service learning offers the explicit benefit of achieving learning goals. Unlike an internship, service learning addresses the interests and voice of the community partner. Service learning strives for mutuality, balancing the focus on student learning and the community's interests.[11]

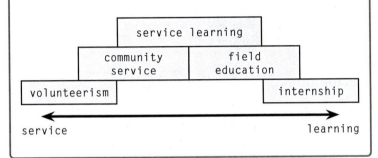

dark out of fear for her safety while her male friends do not experience such restrictions. Or consider how a person of color might surprise a white friend by recalling instances of being stopped and questioned by police officers for no apparent reason.

Volunteering does not necessarily disrupt social inequalities to achieve its purpose. In fact, it may reinforce social inequalities if the volunteer is perceived or perceives herself to have the resources, solutions, and power to address social problems. When service is understood as a way to fulfill an unmet need of the community or remedy a community problem, the primary focus going into the community can be on the need or the problem. This can deflect the student's attention from the community's strengths and resources. John McKnight and John Kretzmann offer a helpful tool to avoid

---

11. Andrew Furco, "Service Learning: A Balanced Approach to Experiential Education," in *Introduction to Service-Learning Toolkit: Resources for Faculty* (Providence, RI: Campus Compact, 2001), 10.

focusing on a community's deficiencies. In their model of "Asset-Based Community Development," they suggest empowering communities to identify the resources and skills that already exist in their neighborhoods and building on those strengths.[12] This approach to service is particularly helpful in service learning because it not only empowers the community but it also helps the learner gain a more adequate understanding and appreciation of the community.

Effective service learning challenges social inequalities by evoking critical reflection on the dynamics of privilege and marginalization within the service-learning relationship and within one's own identities. Acknowledging how one has benefitted from social inequalities can be difficult and is often met with puzzlement, denial or guilt. However, this process is essential for imagining how *everyone* benefits from social justice.

Becoming an Ally for Social Justice

Once people recognize their privilege, they can decide to work alongside marginalized groups as an ally. Reflecting on how college students become allies for social justice, Keith Edwards explores how motivation influences the process.[13] It is helpful to examine one's motivation for service learning because it can influence how one sees and relates to the community.

Edwards observes three ways people are motivated to become allies with marginalized communities. Self-interest motivates some people. For example, a person may decide to become an ally because he or she sees how a friend or family member is treated unjustly. Consider how one might stand up for a friend or loved one hurt by a homophobic remark, but not necessarily work to dismantle the roots of homophobia in society. While this might serve as a starting point for empathy that can motivate social change, the danger is that the self-interested ally might focus solely on the experience of their loved one and fail to see the systemic problem behind the unjust treatment.

---

12. John L. McKnight and John P. Kretzmann, *Building Communities from the Inside Out: A Path Toward Finding and Mobilizing a Community's Assets* (Chicago: ACTA Publications, 1993).

13. Keith Edwards, "Aspiring Social Justice Ally Identity Development: A Conceptual Model," in *NASPA Journal* 43, no. 4 (2006), 39–60.

The second type of ally is motivated by altruism. The altruistic individual wants to help members of oppressed groups because he or she sees the injustice behind social inequalities. This ally might experience discomfort or guilt over his or her privilege, having realized a common humanity with people across social divisions. When one feels guilty, however, one can also become easily defensive. Imagine a service learner who becomes confused and angry when a client is rude to her after she has just served him a meal. As an altruistic ally, she sees herself as giving freely to help a less fortunate individual and expects the other party to treat her with gratitude and respect.

An ally for social justice is motivated not only by the desire to help others but also the conviction that creating a just society benefits everyone, including herself. Edwards uses the language of combined selfishness to explain this motivation, observing how the ally for social justice works alongside marginalized communities to eliminate social inequalities that harm both dominant and oppressed groups. Especially in a context that celebrates altruistic volunteerism, self-interested motivation might seem like a bad thing. However, if one begins with the assumption that people are interdependent, it becomes apparent that everyone is harmed by injustice. This model aligns well with Catholic social thought, which assumes everyone is interdependent because people are social by nature.

When reflecting on ally-identity development, it is important to consider the multiple identities that influence an individual and that person's relationships to various communities. Intersectionality is a concept that refers to the reality that one experiences oneself as a member of multiple social groups at the same time. One's gender, race, ethnicity, socioeconomic class, nationality—all interact to influence one's experience of privilege and marginalization. Edwards considers this in his stages of development, pointing out that one may come to see oneself as an ally for social justice and at the same time develop critical consciousness of one's own oppression.[14] For example, in his service-learning experience a Latino man might grow as an ally to women after encountering and reflecting upon sexism while also becoming more aware of how he has been impacted by white dominance. Within a given classroom, as within a given individual,

---

14. Ibid., 54.

privilege and power are complex realities influencing how one relates to a community and envisions social justice.

Tips for Becoming an Ally for Social Justice

Blame the system not the individual. An ally for social justice recognizes how social structures advantage some while disadvantaging others. This reality complicates attempts to assign personal responsibility for societal problems.

Do not let guilt be a barrier to growth. An ally for social justice welcomes the opportunity to unmask their own privilege and unconscious biases as a process of their own liberation.

Continue to envision the common good. Recognizing that we are all interdependent, an ally for social justice sees how everyone benefits from transforming unjust social conditions.

See-Judge-Act and the Catholic Social Tradition

In 1961, Pope John XXIII identified in *Mater et magistra* (*Christianity and Social Progress*) the process of seeing, judging, and acting as a way to bring the Church's teachings on social matters to bear in concrete situations.

> The teachings in regard to social matters for the most part are put into effect in the following three stages: first, the actual situation is examined; then, the situation is evaluated carefully in relation to these teachings; then only is it decided what can and should be done in order that the traditional norms may be adapted to circumstances of time and place. These three steps are at times expressed by the three words: *observe, judge, act.* (no. 236)

John XXIII presents Catholic social teaching as a set of norms to apply to specific circumstances. This text is designed to help service learners do just that by moving from universal principles to concrete application. The text presents principles drawn from the Catholic social tradition and encourages readers to apply them to issues using the methodology of see-judge-act. By presenting Catholic social thought in this way, the text invites students to discover the meaning and significance of this thought in relation to concrete situations they may be familiar with through service learning.

Chapter 1 provides an overview of the Catholic social tradition and introduces the Catholic Church's official social teachings. The remaining chapters, 2–8, each features a major principle drawn from these teachings. Designed especially for readers engaged in service learning, the chapters provide information and tools for using the principles of Catholic social teaching as a basis for evaluating unjust situations and identifying actions aimed at promoting justice.

CHAPTER

Overview of the Catholic Social Tradition

The Catholic social tradition (CST), broadly understood, refers to the thinking, actions, and teachings that have emerged as members of the Catholic Church have responded to social injustices throughout history. This chapter will briefly discuss Catholic social thought and action and then will explore in more detail the Catholic Church's modern-era social teaching, the teaching that this text invites readers to learn about and apply to social problems encountered in service-learning situations using the see-judge-act process. The chapter will introduce the major documents that comprise CST and explore the sources that inform it, its methodology, and the major principles it articulates.

Catholic Social Thought and Action

Christians have thought about and acted on the implications of the gospel message for their relationships since the beginnings of the church. This message includes a call to Christians to love both God and neighbor: "You shall love the Lord, your God, with all your heart, with all your soul, and with all your mind. You shall love your neighbor as yourself" (Matthew 22:37,39). Christians have wrestled to understand what the love of neighbor means and what actions it demands. Catholic social thought, in its broadest sense, refers to the ongoing reflection on the social implications of Christian discipleship—being a follower of Jesus Christ. Catholic social thought emerges through the work of many people, including Church leaders, theologians, ethicists, leaders of movements for social change, and the many other Catholics and others of good will trying to live out their faith in the world.

Listed here is a small sampling of key figures who have contributed to Catholic social thought and action in recent centuries. These people have worked to bring about a more equitable and just world; in this they epitomize the see-judge-act process.

Wilhelm Emmanuel von Kettler. Von Kettler (1811–1877) was the archbishop of Mainz, Germany, during the emergence of modern Catholic social teaching in Europe. In the aftermath of the Industrial Revolution, he encouraged fellow Catholics to address the social and economic problems of the day. He inspired the work of the Fribourg Union, a predominantly lay Catholic think tank that defended the rights of workers and the right to private property while advocating for an alternative to unfettered capitalism and socialism.

John Ryan. Ryan (1869–1945), a Catholic priest and economist, applied insights of Catholic social teaching to social problems in the United States in the early twentieth century. He taught moral theology at the Catholic University of America and published writings that defended a worker's right to employment, a living wage, and just working conditions. Many of his ideas are also found in Franklin D. Roosevelt's New Deal, which put into place many safety nets still present in American society.

Jacques Maritain. Maritain (1882–1973), a French philosopher influenced by the work of Thomas Aquinas, had a lasting impact on modern Catholic theology and ethics. His writings on human dignity and freedom contributed to the Catholic Church's embrace of human rights and democracy.

Dorothy Day. Day (1897–1980) is regarded by many as one of the most important activists in the history of American Catholicism. Along with Peter Maurin, she established the Catholic Worker movement in 1933 as a way to promote social justice, peace, and simplicity. Her thoughts on nonviolence, hospitality, and solidarity with people living in poverty have made an important contribution to the Catholic social tradition.

Joseph Cardinal Bernardin. Bernardin (1928–1996), a bishop from Chicago, inspired the Catholic Common Ground Initiative, which encourages collaboration among all Catholics on important social and political issues. He challenged Catholics to transcend partisan politics and embrace a consistent ethic of life—an ethic that opposes abortion, the death penalty, war, euthanasia, and poverty by defending human dignity across the entire life span and all circumstances.

Saint Mother Teresa of Calcutta. Mother Teresa (1910–1997), founder of the Missionaries of Charity and winner of the 1979 Nobel Peace Prize, dedicated her life to serving people living in extreme poverty in Calcutta. She consistently related her care for the most vulnerable to her love for Christ.

Cesar Chavez. Chavez (1927–1993) was an organizer who, along with Dolores Huerta, established the National Farm Workers Association in 1962, which became the United Farm Workers union (UFW). Informed by Catholic social thought and moved by the plight of migrant farmworkers in California's Central Valley, Chavez advocated for the dignity of workers and care for the environment. Chavez employed nonviolent tactics such as fasting, strikes, and boycotts in the struggle to secure the rights of workers to fair pay and safe working conditions.

Gustavo Gutierrez. Gutierrez (1928–), a Catholic priest from Peru, is considered by many to be the "father of liberation theology." His theology, which emphasizes God's commitment to the liberation of oppressed people through the transformation of unjust social structures, is rooted in his observation of the reality of poverty in Latin America. Liberation theology's insistence on the preferential option for the poor has made a lasting impact on the Catholic social tradition.

Dorothy Stang. Stang (1931–2005), a Catholic sister from Ohio, spent thirty years in Brazil, advocating for economic justice and environmental sustainability in the Amazon. Her vocal opposition to logging and ranching practices that destroyed the rain forest and displaced local farmers led to her assassination in 2005. She dedicated her life to caring for creation and working for environmental justice.

Helen Prejean. Prejean (1939–) is a Catholic sister and leader in the US movement to abolish the death penalty and reform the prison system. Her advocacy is rooted in her experience ministering to inmates on death row and witnessing their executions.

The ten people highlighted—men and women; young and old; lay, ordained, or vowed members of religious communities—have dedicated themselves to the Catholic social mission in different ways, including through direct service, advocacy, education, prayer, and leadership. Each illuminates multiple expressions of charity and work for justice and highlights the importance of charity and justice work in the Catholic social tradition. For example, Mother Teresa's compassionate service to the impoverished and Gustavo Gutierrez's prophetic truth-telling in the face of oppression have both revealed something about what it means to love one's neighbor. The sampling of people and their contributions also reveals the practical orientation of Catholic social thought. Most of these individuals are remembered not only for their ideas about social justice but also for their actions.

The Catholic social tradition has been shaped by well-known individuals but also by untold numbers of other people whose actions have helped to bring about justice. Many of these people—lay, ordained, and vowed religious—have worked in association with parishes and dioceses and with Catholic movements and organizations. Following is a small sampling of organizations whose work provides examples of Catholic social action.

The Society of Saint Vincent DePaul. Founded in 1833 when French law student Frederick Ozanam gathered a group of lay Catholics together to serve the needs of people living in poverty, this society has grown into an international association of over six hundred thousand men and women who promote charity and social justice by providing food, shelter, clothing, and care to people in need. Since its origin, the Society of Saint Vincent DePaul has emphasized the importance of person-to-person assistance.

Pax Christi. This international organization dedicated to peacemaking originated in France through the initiative of lay Catholics who began gathering together to pray for peace. Pax Christi today offers resources for prayer and spirituality as well as education and advocacy related to peacemaking. It welcomes pacifists and just-war advocates while promoting the rights of conscientious objectors, nonviolent conflict resolution, and disarmament. Website: *www. paxchristi.net*.

The Center of Concern. This center engages in analysis, education, and advocacy for the promotion of social justice. Located in Washington, DC, the center works to influence US policies, especially those impacting global justice. Though it is autonomous, ecumenical, and interreligious, the center began in 1971 through the collaboration of the United States Conference of Catholic Bishops (USCCB) and the Society of Jesus (Jesuits) and is rooted in the Catholic social tradition. Website: *https://www.coc.org.*

Network. Network is a nationally recognized Catholic lobbying group based in Washington, DC, and informed by Catholic social teaching. Network promotes just policies related to immigration, healthcare, the environment, and the economy. It was founded in 1972 following a meeting of US Catholic sisters and continues to draw on the experiences of women religious involved in direct service and social justice work in the United States. Website: *https://networklobby.org/.*

The Ignatian Solidarity Network. This network promotes justice education and advocacy opportunities for people affiliated with Jesuit ministries. Their Ignatian Family Teach-In for Justice attracts more than a thousand participants each year and provides an opportunity to learn, reflect, and advocate for justice on Capitol Hill. Website: *https://ignatiansolidarity.net/.*

Catholic Charities USA. This national association of local charities, which provides basic needs assistance and advocacy for millions of Americans each year, is one of the largest nonprofit organizations in the country. Catholic Charities also works closely with local Catholic parishes and the US bishops to provide adoption services and programs to strengthen families. Website: *https://catholiccharitiesusa.org/.*

Catholic Relief Services (CRS). This organization was founded in 1943 by the USCCB and remains the official humanitarian relief organization of the Catholic Church in the United States. CRS provides international aid in the form of disaster relief, microfinance programs, peacebuilding initiatives, and assistance for communities struggling with food insecurity and HIV/AIDS. Website: *https://www.crs.org/.*

Catholic Climate Covenant. This initiative was launched by the US bishops-sponsored Catholic Coalition on Climate Change in 2009. The Catholic Climate Covenant encourages Catholic individuals and organizations to take the Saint Francis Pledge to pray and learn about the moral dimensions of climate change, to change their lifestyle to promote environmental responsibility, and to advocate for the care for creation. Website: *www.catholicclimatecovenant.org.*

PICO (People Improving Lives through Organizing). Since 1972, PICO has empowered local communities to address root causes of social problems through faith-based community organizing. Started by Father John Baumann, a Jesuit priest from California, the PICO National Network now works with diverse congregations and faith traditions to address issues such as housing, healthcare, education, and immigration reform. Website: *www.piconetwork.org.*

These organizations highlight some of the issues to which Catholics have responded—poverty, violence, global inequalities, and environmental destruction—and some of the ways they have done so. The causes of social problems, such as poverty, are often embedded in the political and economic structures of society, requiring not only immediate attention but also long-term solutions and widespread commitment. Organizations dedicated to social justice can facilitate such action. Bishops' conferences, dioceses, parishes, and Catholic institutions such as universities and hospitals also can facilitate action aimed at furthering justice. The many organizations dedicated to putting Catholic social thought into action extend the reach of the Catholic Church beyond its membership and often present an opportunity to collaborate with Christians who are not Catholic, adherents of other religious and nonreligious groups, and individuals.

Catholic Social Teaching

In addition to thoughts and actions, the Catholic social tradition includes teachings. The term *Catholic social teaching* (*CST*) is commonly used to refer specifically to modern-era teachings issued officially by the Catholic Church, beginning with the social encyclical *Rerum novarum* (*On the Condition of Labor*), promulgated by Pope Leo XIII in 1891. Many of the major writings that make up CST are papal encyclicals, which are substantial letters issued by a pope and intended for wide circulation. Other major writings of CST are issued by groups of bishops, gathered in councils or synods, in conjunction with the pope. There is no official list of documents that make up Catholic social teaching, but there is broad consensus about the writings CST includes. The following list of major documents generally considered to comprise CST provides the Latin and English titles of each document along with the document's date, source, context, and major themes.

- *Rerum novarum* (*On the Condition of Labor*), 1891, Pope Leo XIII. Responding to industrialization and the emergence of capitalism in Europe, Leo XIII defends the right to just wages, fair working conditions, and the formation of workers' unions. Responding to socialism, the pope defends the right to private property and the importance of religion.
- *Quadragesimo anno* (*The Reconstruction of Social Order*), 1931, Pope Pius XI. Writing during the Great Depression and the rise of fascism in Europe, Pius XI argues for subsidiarity as guide for the government to protect the common good (in CST this means the flourishing of all) without overpowering local communities.
- *Mater et magistra* (*Christianity and Social Progress*), 1961, Pope John XXIII. Observing an increasingly interconnected world, John XXIII argues for solidarity between nations. He argues specifically for protection for traditional agricultural workers in the context of rapid economic changes.
- *Pacem in terris* (*Peace on Earth*), 1963, Pope John XXIII. In the context of the global arms race of the 1960s, John XXIII advocates for peace and disarmament. He claims that protecting human rights, which he observes to be embedded in human nature, is the foundation of peace.
- *Gaudium et spes* (*Pastoral Constitution on the Church in the Modern World*), 1965, Second Vatican Council. The council declares that the church and world are linked in human history, and the gospel remains relevant in the modern age as it gives meaning to human existence. The text defends the dignity of the human person against discrimination and modern threats to human life.
- *Populorum progressio* (*The Development of Peoples*), 1967, Pope Paul VI. Recognizing the urgent problem of global inequalities in the aftermath of colonization, Paul VI argues for integral human development that promotes the economic, social, cultural, and spiritual flourishing of all.

- *Octogesima adveniens* (*A Call to Action*), 1971, Pope Paul VI. The pope challenges the world to recognize the roots of inequalities and promote political and economic justice on national and international levels. He invites the church around the world to participate in applying CST to local contexts.
- *Justice in the World*, 1971, Synod of Bishops. Observing structural injustices and revolutionary uprisings in Latin America, the synod promotes the preferential concern for the poor. The synod declares the work for justice to be an essential part of promoting the gospel.
- *Laborem exercens* (*On Human Work*), 1981, Pope John Paul II. Recognizing that both capitalism and communism can diminish workers' dignity, the pope advocates for workers' rights and presents a personalist (person-centered) understanding of work.
- *Sollicitudo rei socialis* (*On Social Concern*), 1987, Pope John Paul II. Observing the widening gap between rich and poor nations, the pope calls for international solidarity. He denounces global economic systems that oppress impoverished nations to benefit the wealthy.
- *Centesimus annus* (*On the Hundredth Anniversary of* Rerum Novarum), 1991, Pope John Paul II. Commemorating *Rerum novarum*, the pope critiques both socialist collectivism for undermining personal freedom and unrestrained capitalism for placing competition above the needs of the impoverished.
- *Caritas in veritate* (*Charity in Truth*), 2009, Pope Benedict XVI. Commemorating *Populorum progressio* (*The Development of Peoples*), Benedict XVI addresses challenges to development in the context of globalization. Specifically, he argues that solidarity and a spirit of gratuitousness are needed to promote economic and environmental justice.
- *Evangelii gaudium* (*On the Proclamation of the Gospel in Today's World*), 2013, Pope Francis. In this Apostolic Exhortation, Francis invites the church to embrace the joy of the Gospel and encounter Christ in the poor. He defends human dignity against a throwaway culture and economic exclusion.
- *Laudato si': On Care for Our Common Home*, 2015, Pope Francis. Using the framework of integral ecology, Francis addresses the

interconnected social, cultural, political, and economic dimensions of the ecological crisis. Francis calls for solidarity with the poor who are disproportionately impacted by climate change.

Catholic social teaching developed and will continue to develop in response to particular social issues, so over time the body of official teaching grows and new insights emerge. Central ideas, however, recur throughout the teachings, as the documents' authors aim to apply fundamental principles to particular historical situations. For example, the principle of human dignity that guided Leo XIII's response to industrialization in 1891 informed Benedict XVI's response to globalization more than one hundred years later.

The remainder of this chapter will explore some of the sources that inform CST, the methodology the authors of CST employ, and major principles CST articulates.

Sources of Catholic Social Teaching

Catholic social teaching is rooted in principles drawn from the Old and New Testaments, the doctrines of the Catholic Church, and the work of theologians. Catholic social teaching, however, has never relied solely on Christian sources, drawing on philosophy and most recently, the social sciences. This section of the chapter will briefly highlight a few of the sources that inform CST—Scripture, theology, and a type of philosophical argumentation known as natural law.

The Second Vatican Council (1962–1965)

The Second Vatican Council, also called Vatican II, was an ecumenical council held from 1962 to 1965. When Pope John XXIII announced his plan to convene the Catholic bishops of the world for a council he used the term *aggiornamento*, an Italian word that means "updating," to describe his hope that the council would renew the Catholic Church and make it more responsive to contemporary realities. The council issued sixteen documents on topics related to the life of the church and its relationship to

continued

> **The Second Vatican Council (1962–1965)** *continued*
>
> the world. Some of the most significant developments at Vatican II include changes in the liturgy (including allowing Mass to be celebrated in the spoken language of the local churches rather than in Latin), greater emphasis on the importance of religious liberty, the need for reconciliation with other Christians, the importance of dialogue with people of other religious traditions, and openness to the wisdom of scientific discovery and secular ideas. *Gaudium et spes* (*Pastoral Constitution on the Church in the Modern World*), generally viewed as part of CST, was one of four major documents, called constitutions because they articulate central teachings or principles, issued by Vatican II.[1]

Scripture

The Christian Scriptures, made up of the Hebrew Bible (Old Testament) and the New Testament, are normative sources of Catholic social teaching. This is because the Catholic Church views the Old and New Testaments as the Word of God. In *Dei verbum* (*Dogmatic Constitution on Divine Revelation*), the Second Vatican Council explains the Catholic view that sacred Scripture is the Word of God, and in sacred Scripture, God speaks through human authors in a "human fashion" (no. 12). Aligned with these two ideas—that Scripture is the Word of God and that the Word is expressed through humans—the Catholic Church rejects fundamentalist understandings of the Bible. In other words, Catholics maintain that the Scriptures are inspired by God and, taken as a whole and interpreted with the help of the Holy Spirit, reveal the truths of the Christian faith. At the same time, because the Scriptures are written by human authors in particular historical moments, the interpretation of Scripture must also consider the human factors expressed in the writings. Biblical scholars use several tools to arrive at a better understanding of these factors including archeology, cultural anthropology, and literary tools.

---

1. The three other major documents are *Lumen gentium* (*Dogmatic Constitution on the Church*), *Dei verbum* (*Dogmatic Constitution on Divine Revelation*), and *Sacrosanctum concilium* (*Constitution on the Sacred Liturgy*).

The authors of CST draw on the Scriptures for insight into fundamental principles, including the meaning of social justice and the nature of the human person in relation to God. One example is John Paul II's use of the Bible to develop an understanding of human work in his encyclical *Laborem exercens* (*On Human Work*).

> When man, who had been created "in the image of God . . . male and female" (Gen 1:27), hears the words: "Be fruitful and *multiply, and fill the earth and subdue* it" (Gen 1:28), even though these words do not refer directly and explicitly to work, beyond any doubt they indirectly indicate it as an activity for man to carry out in the world. Indeed, they show its very deepest essence. Man is the image of God partly through the mandate received from his Creator to subdue, to dominate, the earth. In carrying out this mandate, man, every human being, reflects the very action of the Creator of the universe. (no. 4)

Pope John Paul II interprets the biblical story of creation to articulate the relationship between human nature and work. Referring to the mandate to subdue the earth, the pope suggests that work is one of the ways that humanity participates in the creative activity of God and therefore manifests God's image in the world. In the pope's reading, the biblical text is understood in light of the whole story of creation, which highlights the unique ability of humanity to reflect God's image. The pope draws on the Bible in this case to argue for the dignity of work.

Gender Inclusive Language and Church Documents

English translations of magisterial documents often refer to humanity as *man* and use male pronouns when speaking of both men and women. This book uses gender-inclusive language whenever possible but follows the translation offered by the Vatican, which often lacks such inclusivity.

Theology

Christian theology, grounded in Scripture, the Christian tradition, and the experiences of Christians, is also a source for Catholic social teaching. The classic definition of theology offered by Saint Anselm (1033–1109) is "faith seeking understanding." This definition reveals two important dimensions of theology. First, theology presupposes the experience of faith and seeks to understand the object of faith—God. Theology is not limited to reasoning about God. Second, theology tries to make sense of reality in light of belief in God. Professional theologians take up in a more systematic way what many people of faith do throughout their lives. When individuals reflect on a significant experience such as falling in love or suffering an injury or on an aspect of nature or themselves in light of Christian belief, they sometimes come to new understandings of their faith. This reflection is called *theologizing*. The work of theology is never ending because human beings continue to reflect on experiences in light of Christian faith.

One example of theology informing Catholic social teaching can be found in the way that Vatican II's *Gaudium et spes* (*Pastoral Constitution on the Church in the Modern World*) defines the human person.

> The root reason for human dignity lies in man's call to communion with God. From the very circumstance of his origin man is already invited to converse with God. For man would not exist were he not created by God's love and constantly preserved by it; and he cannot live fully according to truth unless he freely acknowledges that love and devotes himself to His Creator. (no. 19)

A theological understanding of the human person is different from nontheological understandings because theology tries to make sense of human existence in light of faith in God. In *Gaudium et spes*, the origin, purpose, and meaning of the human person is understood in relationship to God. These theological assumptions inform how the Catholic Church understands human dignity, resulting in different perspectives on human dignity than might be found in other approaches.

Natural Law Philosophy

Traditionally, philosophy has been an important source for Catholic thought, particularly a form of philosophical argumentation known as *natural law*. A natural law argument begins with the assumption that through the use of reason, the human mind is capable of discerning God's will in creation. Following this assumption is the claim that people's actions should conform to the order of creation as observed in the natural world and common human experience. For example, the natural inclination to preserve one's life can be used to develop a moral mandate against suicide. The advantage of a natural law argument is that it transcends religious and cultural differences. For instance, the Catholic Church uses natural law argumentation to claim the universal significance of certain teachings such as the insistence on universal human rights. The following excerpt from Pope John XXIII's encyclical on peace, *Pacem in terris* (*Peace on Earth*), provides another example of natural law informing Catholic social teaching.

> All created being reflects the infinite wisdom of God. It reflects it all the more clearly, the higher it stands in the scale of perfection. But the mischief is often caused by erroneous opinions. Many people think that the laws which govern man's relations with the State are the same as those which regulate the blind, elemental forces of the universe. But it is not so; the laws which govern men are quite different. The Father of the universe has inscribed them in man's nature, and that is where we must look for them; there and nowhere else. (nos. 5–6)

The pope expresses the idea that God has ordered human nature, and this order should govern human relationships. From this perspective, peace will be achieved by transcending differences of opinion and following the laws of human nature.

One of the limitations of natural law is that it can fail to take into account historical and cultural differences that shape understandings of human nature. With the shift to a more historically conscious approach to theology and ethics in the second half of the twentieth century, Catholic thinkers have relied less on natural law.

Many insights of natural law, however, particularly the claim that there are universal aspects of human nature, continue to inform Catholic social teaching.

Methodology of Catholic Social Teaching

In *Gaudium et spes* (*Pastoral Constitution on the Church in the Modern World*), the Second Vatican Council identified the significance of history in shaping social life and described the Catholic Church's task as reading or "scrutinizing the signs of the times and of interpreting them in the light of the Gospel" (no. 4). The signs of the times[2] are significant events, developments, struggles, and opportunities that characterize an era. The methodology of reading the signs of the times requires an ongoing process of understanding the world and discerning how to think and act in response to what is happening. Reading the signs of the times—a process with a close affinity to the see-judge-act process because both involve social analysis, ethical reflection, and informed action—is a helpful way to think about the methodology that has spurred the development of CST.

Recognizing the diverse social situations that exist in the world, in *Octogesima adveniens* (*A Call to Action*), Pope Paul VI instructs local churches to carry out a process of reading the signs of the times, or of seeing, judging, and acting, within their own contexts.

> In the face of such widely varying situations it is difficult for us to utter a unified message and to put forward a solution which has universal validity. Such is not our ambition, nor is it our mission. . . . It is up to the Christian communities

---

2. The phrase "reading the signs of the times" has biblical roots, appearing in the Gospel of Matthew (16:1–3): "The Pharisees and Sadducees came and, to test him, asked him to show them a sign from heaven. He said to them in reply, 'In the evening you say, "Tomorrow will be fair, for the sky is red"; and, in the morning, "Today will be stormy, for the sky is red and threatening." You know how to judge the appearance of the sky, but you cannot judge the signs of the times.'" The passage depicts Jesus responding to religious leaders who are skeptical about his teaching authority. In his reply, Jesus challenges them to open their eyes to what is going on around them. He points out that they can read weather patterns in the signs of nature, but they do not recognize signs of God at work in the world—healing the sick, forgiving sinners, comforting those who are suffering.

to analyze with objectivity the situation which is proper to their own country, to shed on it the light of the Gospel's unalterable words and to draw principles of reflection, norms of judgment, and directives for action from the social teaching of the Church. (no. 4)

The process Paul VI describes is useful for individuals and communities seeking to understand and respond to social situations, but it also describes the type of reflection that those who have authored the Catholic Church's official teachings have engaged in.

Principles of Catholic Social Teaching

Catholic social teaching develops a number of recurring themes, which are often referred to as principles. Though no definitive listing of these principles exists, Catholic Church leaders and scholars have developed various listings helpful to those seeking to understand and apply CST.[3] The lists can provide a framework for organizing CST's central ideas, and therefore can facilitate both learning about CST and its application in particular situations.

The organization of the chapter topics in the remainder of this text reflects the list of seven major themes the USCCB articulated in 1997.[4]

The Dignity of the Human Person. The foundation for all of the Church's social teaching and ethical reflection is its theological understanding of the human person: the human person is created in the image and likeness of God. The belief that each person bears the image of God—regardless of characteristics such as race,

---

3. For example, the Pontifical Council for Justice and Peace lists four major principles (human dignity, solidarity, subsidiarity, and the common good) in *The Compendium for the Social Doctrine of the Church* (Libreria Editrice Vaticana, 2004). Social ethicist Thomas Massaro names nine key themes of Catholic social teaching (the dignity of the human person and human rights; solidarity, common good and participation; family life; subsidiarity and the proper role of government; property ownership: rights and responsibilities; the dignity of work, rights of workers, and support for labor unions; colonialism and economic development; peace and disarmament; and option for the poor and vulnerable) in his book *Living Justice: Catholic Social Teaching in Action* (Lanham, MD: Rowman and Littlefield, 2011).

4. See USCCB, *Sharing Catholic Social Teaching: Challenges and Directions* (Washington, DC: USCCB, 1997).

gender, socioeconomic status, physical attributes, intelligence, behavior, or nationality—grounds Catholic social teaching's affirmation of the dignity of every individual. Furthermore, the conviction that every person bears the image of God regardless of his or her actions grounds the Church's defense of the immeasurable worth of each individual, despite their worst actions and beyond their greatest achievements.

Call to Family, Community, and Participation. Grounded in the belief that people are social by nature, Catholic social teaching recognizes that people participate in various communities, including families, neighborhoods, and nations. Because the family provides the primary experience of community for most people, the Catholic Church emphasizes the importance of supporting families.

The Dignity of Work and the Rights of Workers. The Catholic social tradition affirms the dignity of work and the rights of workers, including the right to a living wage and the right to form labor unions. CST has consistently challenged economic systems that exploit people for their labor or place the value of profit over the value of the human person.

Option for the Poor and Vulnerable. The option for those who are poor and vulnerable calls for prioritizing the needs of marginalized people. Social injustices such as poverty that hinder human development create the conditions in which people are prevented from participating in society. The common good, defined in this context by the flourishing of all, cannot be achieved when individuals are excluded. Empowering everyone to participate strengthens the common good and honors human dignity.

Solidarity. Upholding the dignity of all individuals and empowering them to participate fully in community requires solidarity; a recognition that all people are interconnected and a commitment to work for the good of all people. Solidarity affirms the social nature of the human person and the interdependence of creation. As an ethical stance, solidarity goes beyond the observation that people are interconnected to the conviction that people are responsible for one another.

Care for Creation. This theme emphasizes human beings' responsibility toward the whole of creation—human and nonhuman. CST advocates for environmental justice, recognizing that marginalized

people (through situations such as poverty or racism) are disproportionately affected by environmental degradation.

Rights and Responsibilities. The Catholic Church teaches that
human rights flow from human dignity, making them universal and
intrinsic. The Church also teaches that the human person is social by
nature and meant to live in relationship with others. Therefore, the
Church emphasizes responsibilities alongside rights.

Applications of Catholic Social Teaching in the United States

The major writings of CST described earlier in the chapter are
universal in scope, which means the pope or bishops who issued
them intended to speak to the entire church and in some cases the
world. The leaders of local churches are responsible for applying
the universal teachings to situations that arise in local settings. The
USCCB has carried out this responsibility by addressing numerous social, economic, and political issues particular to the United
States. The following list of selected writings illustrates the range
and diversity of topics the USCCB addressed in recent decades
through official statements.

- *Brothers and Sisters to Us, Pastoral Letter on Racism,* 1979
- *The Challenge of Peace: God's Promise and Our Response,* 1983
- *Economic Justice for All,* 1986
- Labor Day Statements, published annually since 1986
- *Renewing the Earth: An Invitation to Reflection and Action on Environment in Light of Catholic Social Teaching,* 1991
- *The Harvest of Justice Is Sown in Peace,* 1993
- *Called to Global Solidarity,* 1997
- *A Fair and Just Workplace: Principles and Practices,* 1999
- *Forming Consciences for Faithful Citizenship,* published before each presidential election since 1999
- *Global Climate Change: A Plea for Dialogue, Prudence, and the Common Good,* 2001
- *A Place at the Table,* 2002

- *"For I Was Hungry and You Gave Me Food": Catholic Reflections on Food, Farmers, and Farmworkers,* 2003
- *Strangers No Longer: Together on a Journey of Hope. A Pastoral Letter Concerning Migration from the Catholic Bishops of Mexico and the United States,* 2003

Looking Ahead

The seven remaining chapters of this text are designed to help service learners understand CST's central principles, gain insight into how these principles have been applied to particular situations by the Catholic Church in the United States, and prepare to apply the principles to situations they are familiar with, using the see-judge-act process.

Each chapter begins by briefly introducing a principle of CST and offering two sets of reflection questions. The questions are designed to help readers identify their prior knowledge, assumptions, and expectations related to the principle and to an issue the chapter will explore in relation to the principle. The questions also invite readers to consider how these may influence what they see in service-learning settings. Next, each chapter presents more detailed information about the principle in CST, and then considers how the USCCB and other Catholic leaders have applied the principle to an issue in the United States. The chapters then discuss current events, social science data, and insights from Christian ethics in order to help readers analyze a contemporary social situation with which they are familiar. A summary follows, then a short vignette drawn from an actual service-learning setting, together with a series of questions designed to help readers practice aspects of the see-judge-act process. The stories featured in the vignettes are told from the perspectives of students, community partners, and faculty members. The details have been changed to protect the anonymity of all parties. The questions encourage readers to use principles of Catholic social teaching to evaluate social situations and actions that might further promote social justice. Each chapter concludes with suggestions for further study.

For Further Study

Printed Materials

Bergman, Roger. *Catholic Social Learning: Educating the Faith That Does Justice.* New York: Fordham University Press, 2010.

Brady, Bernard. *Essential Catholic Social Thought.* Maryknoll, NY: Orbis Press, 2008.

Deberri, Edward, and James Hug. *Catholic Social Teaching: Our Best Kept Secret.* Fourth edition. Maryknoll, NY: Orbis Press, 2003.

Dorr, Donal. *Option for the Poor, Option for the Earth: From Leo XIII to Pope Francis.* Revised edition. Maryknoll, NY: Orbis Press, 2016.

Himes, Kenneth, ed. *Modern Catholic Social Teaching: Commentaries and Interpretations.* Washington, DC: Georgetown University Press, 2005.

Massaro, Thomas. *Living Justice: Catholic Social Teaching in Action.* Lanham, MD: Rowman & Littlefield, 2011.

Mich, Marvin Krier. *Catholic Social Teaching and Movements.* Second printing. Mystic, CT: Twenty-Third Publications, 2000.

———. *The Challenge and Spirituality of Catholic Social Teaching.* Expanded edition. Maryknoll, NY: Orbis Press, 2011.

Websites

Education for Justice, *https://educationforjustice.org/.*

A project of the Center of Concern offering resources for educators and ministers on Catholic social thought including commentaries on documents, reflections on films, and resources for prayer and action.

Defending Human Dignity against Discrimination

Introduction

Catholic social teaching (CST) affirms the innate value and dignity of every person and recognizes that people express their dignity through various social activities, including participating in family life; working; exercising one's civic responsibilities; and expressing one's creativity. CST also recognizes that human dignity can be diminished or obscured when aspects of social life exploit people or suppress their freedom to participate in economic or political life. However, Catholic teaching maintains that even if a person's dignity is overlooked or denied by social conditions, it cannot be taken away. CST aims to promote a society that respects each person by denouncing aspects of social life that disregard human dignity. The *Compendium of the Social Doctrine of the Church* summarizes well the idea that affirming human dignity lies at the center of Catholic social thought.

> *The whole of the Church's social doctrine, in fact, develops from the principle that affirms the inviolable dignity of the human person.* In her manifold expressions of this knowledge, the Church has striven above all to defend human dignity in the face of every attempt to redimension or distort its image; moreover she has often denounced the many violations of human dignity. (no. 107)[1]

---

1. Pontifical Council for Justice and Peace, *The Compendium of the Social Doctrine of the Church* (Libreria Editrice Vaticana, 2004).

Reflect on your understanding of CST's defense of human dignity and, if possible, relate this understanding to a service-learning setting with which you may be familiar. This might include a community organization with which your school has a relationship, a social context in which you serve, the life situation of people with whom you work, or another aspect of service learning.

- How do you define dignity? What is the relationship between dignity and respect? What people, experiences, and beliefs have shaped your understanding of human dignity?
- What does it mean to live with dignity? What social conditions allow people to grow in dignity? What social conditions violate human dignity?
- Identify specific ways you may have seen people expressing and honoring human dignity in a service-learning setting. Also, identify ways you may have seen people diminish or disregard the dignity of others.

Some of the most insidious violations of human worthiness or dignity are rooted in the erroneous belief that certain people are inferior to others because of their race, ethnicity, gender, or sexuality. Such attitudes have given rise to unjust social structures that diminish people's ability to develop their potential and fully participate in society. This chapter will highlight racism, one of the many "isms"—attitudes of superiority such as sexism, classism, ageism, ethnocentrism—that perpetuate social injustice.

Intersectionality and Human Dignity

Threats to human dignity come in many forms. Oppressive attitudes and structures can be built upon classism, racism, sexism, and other injustices. The term *intersectionality* refers to the ways that multiple injustices exist together within communities and individuals. A white cisgender[2] woman, for example, might

continued

---

2. *Cisgender* is a term to describe a person whose gender identity corresponds to their sex assigned at birth.

Intersectionality and Human Dignity *continued*

identify with a marginalized group because of her gender while she also experiences racial privilege. The concept of intersectionality has helped people working for justice to conceptualize their commitments in a way that recognizes difference. For example, contemporary feminists informed by intersectionality recognize that women of color and poor women might organize and understand feminism differently than white middle class women because of interlocking experiences and structures of oppression.

Although the history of the Catholic Church in the United States reveals examples of complacency and even participation with racist structures, the United States Conference of Catholic Bishops (USCCB) today draws on CST to issue a strong critique of racism in the United States. Consider the significance of race in your life and in service-learning sites with which you may be familiar.

- Have you thought about race a lot in your life? Where did you learn about racial differences? What role does it play in your identity and your relationship to others?

- Has a service-learning experience prompted you to think differently about race? If so, has your thinking surfaced any assumptions or challenged any racial stereotypes of which you were unaware?

- Can you identify ways that racism has affected the community in which you live? Have you met people in a service-learning setting who have been affected by racism? If so, have you been able to discern attitudes or structures that perpetuate racism in these contexts?

This chapter introduces the principle of human dignity in CST by tracing the principle's development from the early social encyclical *Rerum novarum* (*On the Condition of Labor*, 1891) to the Second Vatican Council's *Gaudium et spes* (*Pastoral Constitution on the Church in the Modern World*, 1965) and finally to Pope John Paul II's *Evangelium vitae* (*The Gospel of Life*, 1995). Then it highlights how the USCCB has applied CST on human dignity to racism in the Unites

States by analyzing the bishops' pastoral letter *Brothers and Sisters to Us* (1979) and by examining the work of two of the five USCCB subcommittees dedicated to cultural diversity in the Catholic Church. Next, the chapter draws on social science data and the work of a contemporary Catholic ethicist to help service learners begin to analyze and address racism in the United States today. The final section of the chapter provides a summary followed by a vignette drawn from an actual service-learning setting and a series of questions designed to help readers become more familiar with the see-judge-act process.

Human Dignity in Catholic Social Teaching

Early Catholic Social Teaching on Human Dignity

The early social encyclicals evoke the principle of human dignity to argue that human nature demands labor standards. Pope Leo XIII's *Rerum novarum* (*On the Condition of Labor*), for example, advocates for state-enforced labor standards such as fair wages, decent working conditions, and Sunday rest. The pope roots the rights of the worker in God's will rather than the worker's individual interests or desires. He says in *Rerum novarum* (*RN*), for example,

> No man may with impunity outrage that human dignity which God Himself treats with great reverence, nor stand in the way of that higher life which is the preparation of the eternal life of heaven. Nay, more; no man has in this matter power over himself. To consent to any treatment which is calculated to defeat the end and purpose of his being is beyond his right; he cannot give up his soul to servitude, for it is not man's own rights which are here in question, but the rights of God, the most sacred and inviolable of rights. (no. 40)

By emphasizing the "rights of God" over the rights of the person, Leo XIII presented an understanding of human dignity that differed from the liberal human-rights tradition that had emerged out of the European Enlightenment's emphasis on individual freedom and subjectivity. By asserting the authority of human reason and elevating the importance of individual freedom, Enlightenment thinking challenged the authority of the Catholic Church while it laid the foundations of the modern human-rights tradition in the Western world. The early social encyclicals reacted to the perceived threats of modernity by criticizing individualistic understandings of the human person and human rights.

Leo XIII's understanding of human dignity as God-given and therefore intrinsic to human nature echoes throughout CST. The understanding that this notion of human nature is supported by natural law provides a basis for making universal claims about human existence. Like the early social encyclicals, contemporary CST grounds claims about human nature in natural law.

The Second Vatican Council on Human Dignity

Beginning with Pope John XXIII and Vatican II, CST has paid more attention to human subjectivity and freedom. Vatican II speaks of human nature, but it also speaks of the human existence as a mystery, offering a theological understanding of personhood that gives meaning to the principle of human dignity. In *Gaudium et spes* (*Pastoral Constitution on the Church in the Modern World*), Vatican II presents the meaning of human existence in light of a Christian understanding of creation, redemption, and final destiny with God. The text draws on the book of Genesis, placing the human person in a special relationship with God the Creator by asserting that humanity bears God's own image and likeness. *Gaudium et spes* stresses the implications of humanity's likeness to God. The teaching implies that a person is able to know and love God and is therefore responsible for responding to God's invitation to relationship. Christians understand God as the Trinity, with the Father, Son, and Holy Spirit always coexisting in relationship. To bear the image of a relational God implies that people are social beings, not meant to live in isolation. Finally, people reflect the image of God in their freedom to make decisions in a way that the rest of creation cannot. With such freedom comes responsibility for one's decisions.

Gaudium et spes (*GS*) articulates the relationship among freedom, responsibility, and the invitation to relationship with God in its understanding of conscience. Understanding the text's treatment of conscience is essential for grasping the notion of human dignity that emerges from Vatican II.

In the depths of his conscience, man detects a law which he does not impose on himself, but which holds him to obedience. Always summoning him to love good and avoid evil, the voice of conscience when necessary speaks to his heart: do this, shun that. For man has in his heart a law written by God; to obey it is the very dignity of man; according to it he will be judged. Conscience is the most secret core and sanctuary of a man. There he is alone with God, Whose voice echoes in his depths. (no. 16)

This understanding of conscience relates human dignity to an individual's ability to discern right from wrong and make decisions based on one's relationship with God. The council identifies the invitation to relationship with God as the foundation and rationale for the principle of human dignity. "The root reason for human dignity lies in man's call to communion with God" (*GS*, no. 19). Catholic teaching affirms that responding to God's call to relationship requires an exercise of freedom. "Hence man's dignity demands that he act according to a knowing and free choice that is personally motivated and prompted from within, not under blind internal impulse nor by mere external pressure" (*GS*, no. 17). Such an understanding of freedom is not contrary to the obligation to seek the good; rather, a person can find the good only in freedom (*GS*, no. 17).

Drawing on biblical texts, *Gaudium et spes* explains the reality of sin in the world as a result of humanity's misuse of freedom. For this reason, the text explains, "all of human life, whether individual or collective, shows itself to be a dramatic struggle between good and evil" (no. 13). The Christian tradition teaches that, though humanity has weakened its relationship with God through sin, God actively seeks to restore the relationship, offering forgiveness and salvation to humanity. Christian belief in the mystery of the Incarnation, of God becoming human in the person of Jesus Christ, is integral to the Catholic Church's understanding of human dignity. The Catholic tradition maintains that the Incarnation affirmed the goodness of creation, not destroying human nature but perfecting it, "Since human nature as He assumed it was not annulled, by that very fact it has been raised up to a divine dignity in our respect too" (*GS*, no. 22). By highlighting the transcendent orientation of human existence,

Gaudium et spes argues that God provides the ultimate meaning of human existence and the foundation of human dignity.

Within this theological framework, human dignity is established and perfected by God, and therefore cannot be earned or taken away. As a result of human existence, not human achievement, the quality of human dignity implies a fundamental equality in the value of all people. The theological understanding of personhood as presented at Vatican II has implications for the Church's teaching on human rights. *Gaudium et spes* declared, "With respect to the fundamental rights of the person, every type of discrimination, whether social or cultural, whether based on sex, race, color, social condition, language, or religion, is to be overcome and eradicated as contrary to God's intent" (no. 29). With this statement, Vatican II asserts that discrimination is a violation of a person's fundamental rights, which are established by God. This vision of the human person grounds the Church's argument against racism, sexism, classism, and other forms of discrimination.

The Consistent Ethic of Life Since John Paul II

Pope John Paul II built his social encyclicals on the Catholic theological understanding of personhood and the God-given dignity of all people affirmed at Vatican II. Throughout his writings, and particularly in *Evangelium vitae* (*The Gospel of Life*), John Paul II drew on Vatican II's theological understanding of the human person to argue for the need to revere life at all its stages and to highlight that respecting the dignity of all is a social concern.

The pope was convinced that a society's attitude toward the human person can lead to either a culture of life or a culture of death. In *Evangelium vitae* (*EV*), John Paul II states the following:

> It is not only a personal but a social concern which we must all foster: a concern to make unconditional respect for human life the foundation of a renewed society. We are asked to love and honour the life of every man and woman and to work with perseverance and courage so that our time, marked by all too many signs of death, may at last witness the establishment of a new culture of life, the fruit of the culture of truth and of love. (no. 77)

A *culture of life* is supported by a collective attitude that respects human life at all stages and opposes multiple threats to life including abortion, euthanasia, the death penalty, war, violence, and poverty. John Paul II's insight that a society's attitude toward human life at every stage leads to either a life-affirming or death-dealing culture gives rise to a concern for establishing a *consistent ethic of life*. A consistent ethic of life defends human dignity against multiple injustices, recognizing that all threats to human life stem from a distorted understanding of the human person that should be replaced with an uncompromising reverence for life.

A culture of life, as Pope John Paul presents it, not only opposes specific threats to life but it also resists attitudes that obscure the inherent value of each person. He cites individualism and materialism as characteristics of a culture of death. A materialistic and individualistic view of reality, John Paul argues, results in a distorted understanding of the human person that locates a person's value in his or her "usefulness" to society. It is particularly harmful to the most vulnerable members of society.

> In the materialistic perspective described so far, interpersonal relations are seriously impoverished. The first to be harmed are women, children, the sick or suffering, and the elderly. The criterion of personal dignity—which demands respect, generosity and service—is replaced by the criterion of efficiency, functionality and usefulness: others are considered not for what they "are," but for what they "have, do and produce." This is the supremacy of the strong over the weak. (*EV*, no. 23)

A culture of life rejects this model of relationship by valuing *being* over *having* (*EV*, no. 98). By valuing people for who they are rather than what they achieve, John Paul's vision of social justice affirms the innate nature of human dignity. Affirming the innate dignity and worth of the human person allows CST to reject all forms of discrimination.

In his 2018 apostolic exhortation *Gaudete et exsultate* (*On the Call to Holiness in Today's World*), Pope Francis cautions against political ideologies that relativize certain ethical issues over others. Specifically, he argues that the Catholic Church's defense of the poor and the rights of migrants should not be perceived as secondary to bioethical issues. Echoing John Paul II, Francis affirms the sacredness of all lives as the foundation of the Church's moral witness.

Our defense of the innocent unborn, for example, needs to be clear, firm and passionate, for at stake is the dignity of a human life, which is always sacred and demands love for each person, regardless of his or her stage of development. Equally sacred, however, are the lives of the poor, those already born, the destitute, the abandoned and the underprivileged, the vulnerable infirm and elderly exposed to covert euthanasia, the victims of human trafficking, new forms of slavery, and every form of rejection. (*GE*, no. 101)

Affirming the innate dignity and worth of the human person allows CST to reject all forms of dehumanization and discrimination, including racism, the focus of the remaining portion of this chapter.

Joseph Cardinal Bernardin and the Consistent Ethic of Life

The phrase *consistent ethic of life* is most often associated with the work of Joseph Cardinal Bernardin (1928–1996). His teaching emerged alongside movements in the Catholic Church in the United States that advocated for consistency in the Church's public voice on issues such as abortion, the death penalty, nuclear war, and other threats to human life. This movement challenged Catholics and others to put political differences aside and defend human dignity. The movement also invited Catholics to consider how the Catholic Church's defense of human dignity should go beyond prolife activities on behalf of the unborn to include efforts aimed at ending social injustices that diminish the *quality* of human life, such as poverty, violence, and discrimination.

The United States Conference of Catholic Bishops on Racism

With its commitment to human dignity and human rights, the Catholic social tradition opposes racism. Yet, the Catholic Church has participated both in maintaining and dismantling the structures of racism in the United States. History reveals that the Church has perpetuated racial injustices. For example, Catholic clergy and religious orders in the United States owned African American slaves well into the nineteenth century and participated in institutionalized segregation by excluding black people from Catholic colleges and seminaries.[3] European Catholic missionaries participated in the cultural suppression and violent displacement of Native Americans during the colonization of North America.[4] At the same time, history shows that Catholics have led efforts to eradicate racism in the United States. Catholic dioceses, parishes, and religious orders provide numerous services and advocacy efforts for racial minorities today, particularly those living in poverty.

John LaFarge and Thea Bowman Challenge Racism

A number of Catholic individuals stand out in the history of activism for racial justice in the United States. For example, John LaFarge, SJ, a white Jesuit priest, promoted awareness of racial injustices in the 1930s. LaFarge was a leader in developing the Catholic Interracial Council, which focused on eliminating racism through education and collaboration among black and white Catholics. Dr. Thea Bowman (1937–1990), a black Franciscan Sister of Perpetual Adoration, promoted diversity and racial justice in the Catholic Church and society by drawing on the resources of the black community. Bowman is remembered for the ways she promoted the integration of African American songs, art, and traditions into Catholic liturgy.

Thea Bowman

© Photo courtesy of Franciscan Sisters of Perpetual Adoration, www.fspa.org

---

3. For a historical analysis of the Catholic Church and African American experiences, see Cyprian Davis, *A History of Black Catholics in the United States* (New York: Crossroad, 1990).

4. For a historical account of the treatment of Native Americans by Christian missionaries, see George Tinker, *Missionary Conquest: The Gospel and Native American Cultural Genocide* (Minneapolis: Fortress Press, 1993).

This ambivalent legacy of the Catholic Church in the United States is the starting point for the USCCB's contemporary teaching on racism. This section will explore how the USCCB has addressed racism in the United States by focusing on their 1979 pastoral letter, *Brothers and Sisters to Us*. It will also highlight the subsequent work on racism led by the USCCB Committee on Cultural Diversity in the Church.

The United States Conference of Catholic Bishops' Pastoral Letter on Racism

In 1979, the USCCB issued a pastoral letter on racism, *Brothers and Sisters to Us (BSU)*. In the letter the bishops asserted that racism is a sin and a violation of human rights.

> Racism is a sin: a sin that divides the human family, blots out the image of God among specific members of that family, and violates the fundamental human dignity of those called to be children of the same Father. Racism is the sin that says some human beings are inherently superior and others essentially inferior because of races. It is the sin that makes racial characteristics the determining factor for the exercise of human rights. (no. 9)[5]

By naming racism as a social sin and a violation of human dignity, the bishops connected the elimination of racism with the Church's mission to participate in Christ's redemptive work in the world.

In the text, the bishops identify overt and covert features of racism in the United States. Specifically, they note that racial minorities are more likely to be trapped in cycles of poverty.

> Major segments of the population are being pushed to the margins of society in our nation. As economic pressures tighten, those people who are often black, Hispanic, Native American and Asian—and always poor—slip further into

---

5. The paragraph numbers cited for quotes from *Brothers and Sisters to Us* reflect the author's paragraph numbering as the version of the document available on the USCCB website lacks both page and paragraph numbers.

> the unending cycle of poverty, deprivation, ignorance, disease, and crime. Racial identity is for them an iron curtain barring the way to a decent life and livelihood. (no. 6)

The fact that racial minorities in the United States are more likely than white people to live in poverty reveals a connection between racial injustice and economic injustice. The bishops point out that, although enforced segregation has been overcome, making racism less overt, one does not have to look far to see signs of covert or disguised racial segregation in housing, education, and the job market. Racial minorities are excluded from certain neighborhoods and are still underrepresented at most of the best schools and top-paying jobs. These examples suggest that racial discrimination has perpetuated stereotypes and structures and has marginalized groups of people because of their race. The bishops argue that expressions of overt and covert racial discrimination contradict one of the central teachings of Christianity—that people are equally loved by God and therefore should be treated with equal dignity and respect through both individual actions and institutional and structural policies and procedures.

The bishops develop an ethical response to racism by drawing on Scripture and the Catholic Church's tradition. They point to the Exodus story, which tells of God liberating Israel from slavery, to emphasize God's desire for freedom for oppressed people. They highlight Gospel passages that reveal Jesus' commitment to justice for the poor and vulnerable to stress the need for Christians to promote justice for racial minorities. The text also points out that the nature of the Church, understood to be the Body of Christ, is to serve as a sign of unity among humankind. "This is the mystery of our Church, that all men and women are brothers and sisters, all one in Christ, all bear the image of the Eternal God" (*BSU*, no. 27). As a global communion, the Catholic Church is a racially and culturally diverse community.

The USCCB points out that in the United States "all too often the Church in our country has been for many a 'white Church,' a racist institution" (*BSU*, no. 30). The USCCB acknowledges that Catholics too often have failed to participate in the mission of promoting justice through combating racism. They also acknowledge ways in which white Catholics have contributed to the problem of racial injustice: "Each of us as Catholics must acknowledge a share in the mistakes and sins of the past. Many of us have been prisoners of fear and prejudice.

We have preached the Gospel while closing our eyes to the racism it condemns. We have allowed conformity to social pressures to replace compliance with social justice" (*BSU*, no. 31). Such complacency toward racism, they stress, contradicts the mission of the Catholic Church and the Christian understanding of the human person.

After naming the reality of racism and providing a theological and ethical challenge, the bishops offer practical directives for the Catholic Church in the United States to eradicate racism and promote racial justice. These include creating programs to support racial minorities to enter into leadership positions in society and in the Church, celebrating diversity through Catholic worship and liturgy, and ensuring that Catholic institutions manifest just policies and practices for people of all races. They also encourage Catholic leaders to speak out about the problem of racism, and they encourage all Catholics to participate in ecumenical, interreligious, and secular movements that promote racial justice (*BSU*, no. 45).

By identifying specific expressions of racism in the United States and challenging the Catholic Church to eliminate racism, *Brothers and Sisters to Us* stands out as an important contribution to Catholic social thought on racial injustice. The pastoral letter has a number of limitations, however, leaving much work to be done in the promotion of justice for people of color. Specifically, respondents to the text have noted that primarily white Church leaders authored the text and directed it to white Church members. This is implicit in the title, with *us* referring to white Catholics who embrace people of color as *brothers and sisters*.[6] Since the publication of the letter, the bishops have worked to empower racial minorities to exercise leadership within the Catholic Church. The USCCB's five subcommittees on cultural diversity carry out much of this work.

The Committee on Cultural Diversity in the Church

In their pastoral letter on racism, the USCCB made an explicit commitment to promote racial justice in the United States and challenged all Catholics to join them in their effort. They also offered direct guidelines to promote racial justice in policies, liturgical

---

6. Bryan Massingale makes this point in *Racial Justice and the Catholic Church* (Maryknoll, NY: Orbis, 2010), 17.

practices, and the monetary commitments of the Catholic Church. In the years following the publication of *Brothers and Sisters to Us*, the bishops implemented a number of pastoral initiatives aimed at celebrating diversity within the Catholic Church and eliminating racism in the Church and society. Many of these efforts were supported by the USCCB's Committee on Cultural Diversity in the Church. The purpose of the committee is to provide training and resources for advocacy and pastoral care that is attentive to the cultural diversity of the Church. It works with permanent subcommittees that collaborate directly with specific communities to promote their interests. There are subcommittees for African American Affairs; Asian and Pacific Affairs; Hispanic Affairs; Native American Affairs; and the Pastoral Care of Migrants, Refugees, and Travelers. Due to limited space, this chapter focuses on only two of the five subcommittees. Specifically, this section examines a small portion of the work of the subcommittee on African American Affairs and the subcommittee on Native American Affairs to provide examples of the USCCB's ongoing work and to highlight some of the challenges the Catholic Church faces today in the effort to promote awareness and respect for diversity in the Church.

Subcommittee on African American Affairs

On the twenty-fifth anniversary of *Brothers and Sisters to Us*, the USCCB's subcommittee on African American Affairs presented a report on the document's effectiveness. The report noted that though some progress has been made in realizing the Catholic Church's commitment to eliminating racism, "much work remains to be done."[7] The report noted that "the majority of American Catholics have not heard the topic of racism addressed in homilies at Mass in the past three years."[8] The report also noted that the enrollment of African American students at Catholic schools declined by fifty thousand students in the twenty-year period between 1984 and 2004

---

7. USCCB, "A Research Report Commemorating the Twenty-Fifth Anniversary of *Brothers and Sisters to Us*: Executive Summary," 12. Available at *http://www.usccb. org/issues-and-action/cultural-diversity/african-american/upload/25th-Ann-Executive-Summary.pdf*. The bishops formed an ad hoc committee against racism in August 2017 with the intention to release a pastoral statement in 2018.

8. Ibid., 2

and that racial segregation at Catholic schools is often higher than that of public schools.[9] The bishops challenge Catholic leaders to "renew their commitment to speak out against racism so as to raise people's awareness of the systemic nature of this form of evil."[10]

One of the findings that troubled the committee was a lack of attention to the formation of religious leaders to serve culturally diverse churches. Studies of seminary programs in the United States showed that "many diocesan seminaries and ministry formation programs are inadequate in terms of their incorporation of the history, culture, and traditions of Black Americans."[11] This can lead to a weak relationship between religious leaders and the people they serve. The committee also suggests that it hinders the promotion of vocations among racial minorities in the Catholic Church because "black men and women, both young and old, seek in their formation programs evidence of the same culture, traditions, and liturgical styles found in their home parishes."[12] In response to its findings, the committee advocated "inculturated ministry formation" so that leaders in the Church can effectively promote the incorporation of spiritual and cultural gifts of minorities into the liturgy.[13]

The term *inculturation* in this context refers to the process by which the ministries of the Catholic Church are carried out in conversation with the cultural realities of a particular community. Attention to the dignity of diverse cultures has grown in the Church since the Second Vatican Council, in *Ad gentes* (*Decree on the Missionary Activity of the Church*, 1965), stated that "The Church, in order to be able to offer all of them [non-Christians] the mystery of salvation and the life brought by God, must implant herself into these groups for the same motive which led Christ to bind Himself, in virtue of His Incarnation, to certain social and cultural conditions of those human beings among whom He dwelt" (no. 10). Understanding the Catholic Church's mission through an incarnational framework has shifted the Church's approach to missionary activity by giving attention to the goodness in local traditions, spiritualities, and cultural

---

9. Ibid., 9–10.

10. Ibid., 12.

11. Ibid., 5.

12. Ibid.

13. Ibid., 7.

practices. In this framework, announcing the gospel does not devalue local cultures. This awareness has been important in developing appreciation for cultural diversity and challenging the tendency to view the manifestation of the Catholic Church in Europe as normative across cultures.

Subcommittee on Native American Affairs

Reconciling with colonial history has been a significant theme in the work of the USCCB's subcommittee on Native American Affairs. In preparation for the fifth centenary of European presence in North America, the USCCB issued a statement, "1992: A Time for Remembering, Reconciling, and Recommitting Ourselves as a People." In the text, the bishops restated their regret for the ways the Catholic Church failed to respect and protect the culture, traditions, and dignity of Native American people during European expansion in North America. The statement acknowledged that injustice toward Native Americans is not just a problem of the past and insisted that "all of us need to examine our own perceptions of Native Americans—how much they are shaped by stereotypes, distorted media portrayals, or ignorance. We fear that prejudice and insensitivity toward native peoples is deeply rooted in our culture and in our local churches."[14]

Recognizing the ways that the Catholic Church has failed to honor the gifts of Native American cultures, the text identifies inculturation as a primary challenge.

> The Church is called to bring the saving word of the Gospel to every people and culture. Our goal must be an authentic inculturation of Catholic faith within the Native American community through a vital liturgical life, continuing educational efforts, and creative pastoral ministry which demonstrate deep respect for native culture and spiritualities and which enhance fidelity to the Catholic faith.[15]

---

14. USCCB, "1992: A Time for Remembering, Reconciling, and Recommitting Ourselves as a People" (November 1991), 3. Available at *http://www.usccb.org/issues-and -action/cultural-diversity/native-american/resources/upload/a-time-for-remembering.pdf.*

15. Ibid., 4.

The text states that the challenge of inculturation must be met by increased participation of Native Americans in all areas of the Church's ministry. The text notes that increasing participation of historically marginalized groups requires empowerment of those communities, which can occur in many ways but must begin with listening to the interests, aspirations, and needs of the immediate community.

The Kateri Tekakwitha Conference

Founded in 1939, the Kateri Tekakwitha Conference promotes cultural awareness and advocacy for Native American Catholics. Named after the first Native North American saint, the conference promotes leadership among Native Americans in the Catholic Church. The conference also promotes inculturation through liturgies that incorporate Native American language, music, and ritual and through meaningful catechesis that is sensitive to Native American identities and traditions.

Reading the Signs of the Times: Racial Discrimination and White Privilege

This section will further examine racism in the United States today by highlighting the contemporary struggle against racism and white supremacy along with analysis by Catholic ethicist Bryan Massingale, whose work applies Catholic social thought to this issue. This section will present the concepts of white privilege and social sin as tools for observing, understanding, and critiquing racism as a structural and cultural injustice in the United States.

In the fall of 2014, protestors gathered in Ferguson, Missouri, a suburb of St. Louis, chanting, "hands up, don't shoot." Many of the protestors believed these to be the final words of Michael Brown, a black teenager shot and killed by a white police officer on August 9, 2014. Although witnesses disputed details of the events surrounding Brown's death, the results were tragic—the unarmed teenager was fatally shot. The Jesuit St. Louis University, along with the Archdiocese's Human Rights Commission, joined other community leaders in advocating for racial justice and accountability.[16] The St. Louis County grand jury did not indict the police officer involved, reinforcing for many the racial injustice perpetuated by the criminal justice system in the United States.[17]

Brown's death was one of the events that gave rise to the Black Lives Matter Movement. The activists behind Black Lives Matter advocate for criminal justice reform, pointing to the systemic nature of police killings of young men of color. In February 2017, a study published by the *American Journal of Public Health* found significant racial disparities in the use of force by police officers. The author found that Black, Hispanic, and American Indian/Alaska Native men were disproportionately represented among young men who died from police force between 2010 and 2014.[18] This study, consistent with previous research, illustrates the systemic reality of racism.

Despite such evidence pointing to the systemic nature of racism, polls show remarkable differences between white and black Americans when it comes to perceptions of racism in the United States. In a 2016 survey the Pew Research Center found that 88 percent of black adults think the country needs to change in order to promote equal rights for blacks. The same survey found that 53 percent of white adults expressed the same view about racial equality.[19]

Black theologian and Catholic priest Bryan Massingale explains the ambivalence that many white people have toward racial justice through the concept of *white privilege*. Examining white privilege requires a shift in attention away from the ways that racism *disadvantages* people of color and instead focuses on how racial injustice

---

16. Colleen Dulle, "If St. Louis is the 'New Selma,' what role will Catholics play in racial reconciliation?" in *America* (October 3, 2017), *https://www.americamagazine.org/politics-society/2017/10/03/if-st-louis-new-selma-what-role-will-catholics-play-racial*.

17. Larry Buchanan, Ford Fessenden, K.K. Rebecca Lai, Haeyoun Park, Alicia Parlapiano, Archie Tse, Tim Wallace, Derek Watkins and Karen Yourish, "Q&A What Happened in Ferguson?" in *The New York Times* (August 10, 2015), available at *https://www.nytimes.com/interactive/2014/08/13/us/ferguson-missouri-town-under-siege-after-police-shooting.html?mcubz=0&_r=0https://www.theguardian.com/us-news/2017/jan/17/black-lives-matter-birth-of-a-movement*.

18. James Buehler, MD, "Racial/Ethnic Disparities in the Use of Lethal Force by US Police, 2010–2014," in *The American Journal of Public Health* (February 2017) available at *http://ajph.aphapublications.org/doi/full/10.2105/AJPH.2016.303575*.

19. Pew Research Center, "On Views of Race and Inequality, Blacks and Whites Are Worlds Apart" (June 27, 2017), available at *http://www.pewsocialtrends.org/2016/06/27/on-views-of-race-and-inequality-blacks-and-whites-are-worlds-apart/*.

sets up *advantages* for white people. Massingale offers concrete examples such as redlining, the practice of designating certain neighborhoods based on racial demographics as high-risk lending zones, making it nearly impossible for people of color to obtain a mortgage. In the 1940s and 1950s, when the Federal Housing Administration offered low-cost loans to promote home ownership, the vast majority of the loans went to white people, enabling them to accumulate assets that they could pass on to their children.[20] In her classic essay, "White Privilege: Unpacking the Invisible Knapsack," Peggy McIntosh proposes a number of examples of white privilege. As a white person, she observes, "I can, if I wish, arrange to be in the company of people of my race most of the time. . . . I am never asked to speak for all the people of my racial group. . . . I can take a job with an affirmative action employer without having coworkers on the job suspect that I got it because of race."[21]

Coming to terms with white privilege is crucial for overcoming the power imbalances that are engendered by racism, but it is not an easy process. Massingale observes,

> Being racially advantaged might be unwanted or undesired by individual white Americans. In fact, some white Americans are distressed when they become aware of the reality of white privilege. Regardless of an individual's desires, an 'invisible package of unearned assets' is enjoyed by white people because of the racial consciousness that is subtly pervasive in our social customs and institutions.[22]

Massingale challenges the Catholic Church to do more to address racism on a pastoral level and in official teachings. In his reading of the bishops' statements on racism since *Brothers and Sisters to Us*, Massingale suggests that "the dominant approach found in recent Catholic episcopal reflection on racism is marked by (1) stress on its interpersonal manifestations; (2) a strategy of moral suasion and appeals to an enlightened conscience; and (3) calls for decency,

---

20. Bryan Massingale, *Racial Justice and the Catholic Church* (Maryknoll, NY: Orbis, 2010), 37–40.

21. Peggy McIntosh, "White Privilege: Unpacking the Invisible Knapsack," *Peace and Freedom* (July 1989): 10–12.

22. Massingale, *Racial Justice*, 37.

civility, respect, and fair treatment, which will translate into improved social relationships among America's racial groups."[23] What is lacking, Massingale argues, is an examination of racism on a cultural level. Culture carries the beliefs, symbols, and stories by which a community gives meaning to its experience and passes on that shared meaning to future generations. Addressing racism on a cultural level requires challenging deeply held beliefs and reshaping the systems that perpetuate these beliefs. With the exception of a few bishops, Massingale notes that the official Catholic response to racism emphasizes the need to change attitudes and personal behavior and is missing an analysis of the systems that structure racial inequalities.

Massingale stresses the "systemic nature" of racism and notes that racism is not limited to the sins of individuals; it exists within the very fabric of society, embodied in systems that disadvantage and oppress people of color. Theologians, including Massingale, join the USCCB in identifying racism as a *social sin*. Social sin is not the same as personal sin, which emerges out of the freedom and responsibility of an individual; therefore, social sin requires a different framework to understand and address it. Social sin, however, is rooted in human decisions and so cannot be separated from personal sin. Because social sin is larger than personal sin, it requires social as well as individual change. Describing social sin, Massingale states, "Social institutions and processes are not morally neutral; they reflect the values and the biases of those who create and maintain them."[24] It can be challenging to identify social sin because, as Massingale continues, "we are then born into a world already formed by these structures, and we grow up thinking that these structures and the values that they incarnate are perfectly normal and legitimate. One of the characteristics of social sin, then, is that we're often blind to its existence."[25] Massingale's work suggests that efforts to eradicate racism should consider the need for societal and ecclesial transformation in addition to personal transformation.

---

23. Bryan Massingale, "James Cone and Recent Catholic Episcopal Teaching on Racism," *Theological Studies* 61:4 (December 2000): 714.

24. Bryan Massingale, "Are You a Social Sinner?" interview with *U.S. Catholic*, *U.S. Catholic* 70, no. 2 (February 2005): 21.

25. Ibid.

Summary and Integration for Service Learners

The social analysis highlighted in this chapter shows that racism continues to affect social structures and cultural attitudes in the United States. Today, the USCCB draws on CST to promote racial justice in the Catholic Church and in society as a whole through teaching, service, and advocacy. CST's principle of human dignity grounds the Church's opposition to racism. This principle, as developed in the Catholic social tradition, invites an uncompromising recognition of the value of each person as a reflection of God's own image.

Now that you have read about the Catholic Church's understanding of human dignity, revisit your answers to the questions at the start of the chapter. Would you answer any questions differently? Does the chapter's discussion of racism in the United States shed light on social issues you may have encountered in a service-learning setting? How can the principle of human dignity help address racial injustices? Use the following service-learning vignette and questions to practice the see-judge-act process in relation to this topic.

See, Judge, Act in the Community

Vignette

Miguel is a community organizer who works with local faith communities to identify their interests and work for social change. He invites service-learners to get to know the congregations and learn about faith-based community organizing.

Miguel has been working with an ecumenical coalition to raise awareness about the impact of gun violence on communities of color. The group recently organized a vigil for an unarmed Latino man who was shot by the police when the officers mistook his Taser for a gun. The incident raised public concern over the number of police shootings and the disproportionate shootings of people of color. Many residents wanted the officers to be charged for excessive use of force but the district attorney did not press charges, saying the officers were acting according to police protocol. Miguel would like to see more de-escalation training for officers and greater accountability for police who use deadly force. He still regards the vigil as a success because it raises awareness of racial injustice and mobilizes the community around criminal justice reform.

See: Social Analysis

- Consider the ways power is held and exercised in the vignette—the community, the shooting victim, the police officers, the organizers. How does power function in the scenario to either diminish or enhance human dignity?
- Would you describe the vigil as a success—why or why not? How would one measure whether the efforts of the community organizers effectively raised awareness of racial injustice?

Judge: Ethical Reflection

- What are some obstacles to achieving the common good in the vignette? How do you see the role of faith-based community organizing in building up the common good?
- How might the concept of *social sin* aid one's understanding of and judgments about racism? What are some of the characteristics of social sin that could be relevant in judging the scenario?

Act: Promoting Justice

- Identify actions aligned with CST's emphasis on the God-given dignity of all people that respond to the situation of people of color suffering from poverty and violence spurred by racism.
- Following Massingale's cultural analysis of racism, what specific actions can be taken by individuals and by communities to counter racism and promote equity and inclusion?

Suggestions for Further Social Analysis in a Service-Learning Context

- Research racial demographics in a selected city according to neighborhood. Do the data suggest the presence of racial segregation?
- Use census information to identify connections between race and other demographic information—income, education level, and employment—in a particular locale. Do the data suggest any connections between race, income, education level, and employment?

• Identify public and private organizations that address racial inequalities in a selected city. What social issues do they target in their promotion of racial equality? What have they identified as some of the obstacles to racial equality?

For Further Study
on Catholic Social Thought and Racism

Cassidy, Laurie and Alexander Mikulich, *Interrupting White Privilege: Catholic Theologians Break the Silence.* Maryknoll, NY: Orbis, 2007.

Catholic Charities, "Poverty and Racism: Overlapping Threats to the Common Good" (January 15, 2008), available at *https://files.catholiccharitiesusa.org/files/publications/Policy-Paper-Poverty-and-Racism.pdf?mtime=20150819174643.*

Copeland, M. Shawn. "Revisiting Racism," *America* 211, no. 1 (July 7, 2014): 21–24.

Flynn, Harry. "In God's Image: Pastoral Letter on Racism" (2003), available at *http://www.archspm.org/pastoral_letters/gods-image-pastoral-letter-racism/.*

George, Francis Cardinal, OMI. "Dwell in My Love: A Pastoral Letter on Racism" (2001).

Massingale, Bryan. *Racial Justice and the Catholic Church.* Maryknoll, NY: Orbis, 2010.

Nothwehr, Dawn M. *That They May Be One: Catholic Social Teaching on Racism, Tribalism, and Xenophobia.* Maryknoll, NY: Orbis, 2008.

Phan, Peter C., and Diana Hayes, eds. *Many Faces, One Church: Cultural Diversity and the American Catholic Experience.* Lanham, MD: Rowman & Littlefield, 2005.

3

CHAPTER

Justice for Immigrants
The Call to Family, Community, and Participation

Introduction

The Catholic social tradition recognizes that people are social by nature and that the organization of society affects how well it protects the dignity of individuals and the ability of people to form community and participate fully in society. Social life provides the context in which people either thrive or encounter obstacles that prevent them from attaining their potential, making it an important topic for Catholic social teaching (CST).

The second of the United States Council of Catholic Bishops' (USCCB) seven themes of CST, the call to family, community, and participation, reflects the Catholic Church's teaching on this topic. This principle has been developed in a number of ways in the Catholic social tradition, emerging in the Church's teaching on the common good, the importance of the family as a basic unit of society, and the need to overcome marginalization by allowing everyone to participate in social life. At the heart of this teaching is the conviction that the well-being of an individual is bound to the flourishing of the entire community. The USCCB summarizes the principle in this way:

> The person is not only sacred but also social. How we organize our society—in economics and politics, in law and policy—directly affects human dignity and the capacity of individuals to grow in community. Marriage and the family

are the central social institutions that must be supported and strengthened, not undermined. We believe people have a right and a duty to participate in society, seeking together the common good and well-being of all, especially the poor and vulnerable.[1]

Reflect on the experiences, beliefs, and values that have shaped your understanding of community.

- Name the communities with which you identify, such as family, neighborhood, church, school, interest group, team, and nation. How would you order these communities according to their significance in your life? What values and beliefs inform the order?
- What is the nature of your participation in the communities you listed in response to the previous questions? Identify any obstacles that may have prevented you from fully participating in any of these communities.
- Identify specific ways you may have seen the building of community in a service-learning setting. Also, identify ways you may have seen community being diminished and people's participation in community thwarted in a service-learning setting.

This chapter will explore the call to family, community, and participation by examining the Catholic Church's response to issues associated with migration, a reality that can both disrupt social life and lead to new expressions of community. This chapter will focus on the USCCB's response to migration, with particular attention to the collaborative work of the US and Mexican bishops. As this chapter will highlight, the US-Mexico border provides an important context for contemporary social analysis and ethical reflection on migration in the Americas. Consider your beliefs and assumptions about migration using the following questions.

- Does your family's history inform your views on migration? Explain.

---

1. USCCB, "Seven Themes of Catholic Social Thought," available at *http://www.usccb.org/beliefs-and-teachings/what-we-believe/catholic-social-teaching/seven-themes-of-catholic-social-teaching.cfm.*

- What is the significance of citizenship and nationality for you? How do these beliefs inform your position on immigration policy? What values inform your position?
- Have any events in your community or any service-learning settings you may be familiar with led you to examine the situation of immigrants in the United States? If so, did your examination prompt you to think differently about immigrants and the policies that affect immigration patterns and the experiences of migrants? Explain.

This chapter will examine how the call to family, community, and participation has developed as a principle of CST by highlighting writings on the common good and family life. Since the early social encyclicals, CST has insisted that people are obligated to promote the common good. Specifically, the first section of this chapter will explore how the principle informs Popes Leo XIII and Pius XI's positions on private property and supports Pope John XXIII's argument for global solidarity.

With a basic understanding of the common good, the chapter will turn to the role of the family in strengthening community life. Pope John Paul II, in particular, highlighted the social dimension of the family and, using the principle of subsidiarity, suggested that strengthening families contributes to the common good from the bottom up. In the next section, the chapter will draw on the joint pastoral letter of the US and Mexican bishops to explore their application of CST to the topic of migration in the context of the Americas. Next, the chapter will highlight some of the realities migrants face, drawing upon the scholarship of Catholic theologian Daniel Groody to analyze the impact of immigration policies on youth and families. The final section of the chapter provides a summary followed by a story of social change and a series of questions designed to help readers practice aspects of the see-judge-act process.

The Call to Family, Community, and Participation in Catholic Social Teaching

Early Social Encyclicals Oppose Individualism and Collectivism

Throughout its history, CST has defended the dignity of the individual and called for meeting the needs of the community. These commitments are reflected in the Catholic social tradition's rejection of individualism—a system in which individual rights supersede community needs—and collectivism—a system of collective control over political and economic matters—in favor of an approach to social life that balances the rights and freedoms of the individual and the needs and interests of the community. This stance provides the foundation for the Catholic Church's teaching on the common good.

The early social encyclicals developed an understanding of the common good in response to the two dominant systems of the Industrial era—liberal capitalism and socialism. Pope Leo XIII critiqued liberal capitalism for promoting excessive individualism at the expense of the needs of the community. The pope also rejected the socialist alternative in fear that too much state control would promote excessive collectivism and threaten the right to private property. The concept of the common good emerges within this concern for the natural right to private property. Following his predecessor, Pope Pius XI used the principle of the common good to argue for the just limitations on private property for the sake of the community. He explained in *Quadragesimo anno* (*The Reconstruction of Social Order*, 1931) that CST defends

> . . . the twofold character of ownership, called usually individual or social according as it regards either separate persons or the common good. For [Pope Leo and Church theologians] have always unanimously maintained that nature, rather [sic] the Creator Himself, has given man the right of private ownership not only that individuals may be able to provide for themselves and their families but also that the goods which the Creator destined for the entire family of mankind may through this institution truly serve this purpose. (no. 45)

Pius XI's understanding of the common good is grounded in the conviction that there is a universal purpose for created things, namely, to sustain the whole human family. This view leaves room for personal and social ownership of property. The common good refers to those goods that contribute to the thriving of the whole community. Pius XI, like Leo XIII, argues that everyone has a responsibility to foster the common good and that the state is obligated to protect the common good.

Pope John XXIII and Vatican II: The Global Common Good

Pope John XXIII builds on the foundation of the early social encyclicals by defending both the dignity of the individual and the importance of community. Writing in the 1960s, John XXIII demonstrated a heightened awareness of the global dimensions of the human community—an awareness with implications for understanding the common good. In his social encyclical *Mater et magistra* (*Christianity and Social Progress*, 1961), he pointed out that nations are increasingly interconnected. He referred specifically to the international economy, arguing that it should be regulated according to the demands of the global common good. He also suggested specific demands for individual nations and the international community. The demands of the common good on the national level include demands that nations foster as much employment as possible, eliminate inequalities, and evaluate progress in light of future generations. In *Mater et magistra* (*MM*), John XXIII states that the common good demands that the international community avoid excessive competition and promote economic growth for developing countries (nos. 79–80).

Reflecting the thought of John XXIII, the Second Vatican Council assumes an interdependent world that transcends nations. *Gaudium et spes* (*Pastoral Constitution on the Church in the Modern World*, 1965) discusses the implications of this reality for the common good.

> Every day human interdependence grows more tightly drawn and spreads by degrees over the whole world. As a result the common good, that is, the sum of those conditions of social life which allow social groups and their individual members relatively thorough and ready access to

their own fulfillment, today takes on an increasingly universal complexion and consequently involves rights and duties with respect to the whole human race. Every social group must take account of the needs and legitimate aspirations of other groups, and even of the general welfare of the entire human family. (no. 26)

Following Vatican II, CST attended to the universal complexion of the common good. This focus affects the Church's position on issues such as international development, human rights, the environment, and migration. Regarding migration, CST maintains that the common good transcends borders but that this does not mean that nations do not have the right and responsibility to regulate their borders and provide security for their citizens. According to *Gaudium et spes* (*GS*), this right, however, cannot override the responsibility to protect the "needs and legitimate aspirations of other groups" (no. 26).

Pope John Paul II on Subsidiarity and the Family

CST calls for the various levels and units of social life—family, neighborhood, town, county, state, nation—to relate according to the principle of subsidiarity. This principle calls for larger social units to solve problems and make decisions for smaller social units only if the smaller unit is unable to do so. If a smaller unit cannot or does not achieve the necessary goods to thrive, the larger community has a responsibility to take action.

In *Familiaris consortio* (*On the Role of the Christian Family in the Modern World*, 1981) Pope John Paul II draws on the principle of subsidiarity to argue for the protection of the privacy and legitimate autonomy of the family in society. According to *Familiaris consortio* (*FC*), "By virtue of this principle, the State cannot and must not take away from families the functions that they can just as well perform on their own or in free associations; instead it must positively favor and encourage as far as possible responsible initiative by families" (no. 45). John Paul II grounds this argument in the conviction that the family is the basic cell of society, because it provides the most immediate experience of relationship. Ideally, the family prepares people to participate in society by instilling the virtues necessary for social life. Family life can teach people about their responsibility toward others, and promote the virtues of solidarity, compassion, and fidelity. Because of this, society should be concerned with promoting healthy families by providing the respect and support they need to thrive. John Paul II suggests the following:

> The family has vital and organic links with society, since it is its foundation and nourishes it continually through its role of service to life: it is from the family that citizens come to birth and it is within the family that they find the first school of the social virtues that are the animating principle of the existence and development of society itself. Thus, far from being closed in on itself, the family is by nature and vocation open to other families and to society, and undertakes its social role. (*FC*, no. 42)

Based on the conviction that the family should be protected as the foundation of a healthy society, John Paul II argues for the legal recognition of specific rights of the family. Among them, he argues that families have "the right to exist and progress as a family," and also "the right to emigrate as a family in search of a better life" (*FC*, no. 46). This understanding of the rights of the family informs the Catholic Church's position on migration, which challenges immigration policies that perpetuate family separation. For this reason, the reunification of families is one of the top priorities in the Church's stance on immigration policies.

Gender, Sexuality, and the Family in *Amoris Laetitia*

In 2014 Pope Francis invited bishops from around the world to gather input from lay Catholics in preparation for the first of two synods on the family. The synod addressed a number of Catholic teachings on the family that have raised theological debates in the modern Church—teachings on women's roles in the family and society, contraception, same-sex marriage, and divorce. The

continued

> **Gender, Sexuality, and the Family** *continued*
>
> broad consultation and synods informed Pope Francis's 2016 apostolic exhortation *Amoris laetitia* (*On Love in the Family*). In the document, Francis offers a theological reflection on the family that celebrates married love and the vocation to parenthood. He identifies pastoral challenges to marriage and family, and instructs religious leaders to respond with mercy to realities such as divorce, recognizing the uniqueness and complexity of individual situations. Responses to the document were mixed, revealing diverse experiences and understandings of gender, sexuality, and marriage within the Church.[2]

The Catholic Church's Response to Immigration to the United States

Church of Immigrants

Immigration has been a concern for the Catholic Church in the United States since it began as a community of immigrants in the eighteenth century and as it grew as waves of Europeans, including Irish, Italians, and Germans, immigrated to the United States in the nineteenth and early twentieth centuries. The Church responded to the needs of immigrants by defending their dignity against xenophobia—fear or hatred of foreigners—and discrimination, advocating for their rights as workers, and providing a space for the celebration of culture in a new context.[3] The European-born immigrants who made up the majority of Catholics in the United States in the early part of the twentieth century faced suspicions that they were unpatriotic. US Catholics were divided on how to articulate that they were both Roman Catholic and American, with so-called "Romanists" advocating for parochial schools and all-Catholic associations and so-called "Americanists" supporting public schools and

---

2. For a collection of diverse responses to *Amoris laetitia*, see *National Catholic Reporter*, "Reactions to Pope's Reflection on Family Life" (April 8, 2016), available at *https://www.ncronline.org/blogs/ncr-today/reactions-pope-s-reflection-family-life*.

3. Jay Dolan, *The American Catholic Experience: A History from Colonial Times to the Present* (Garden City, NJ: Double Day, 1985), 311–14.

collaboration with Protestants in labor unions.[4] The struggles of early Catholic immigrants in the United States, although particular to that time period, highlight some of the primary issues that migrants face today—being vulnerable to exploitation of their labor, facing xenophobia and various forms of discrimination, often having to defend themselves against accusations of being un-American.

The Bishops of the United States and Mexico: *Strangers No Longer*

The Catholic Church in the United States continues to include a large immigrant population but demographics have shifted since the early twentieth century when most Catholic immigrants were from Europe. In 2017 most of the US immigrant population was from Mexico, followed by China and India.[5] Between 2007 and 2015, the number of immigrants from Honduras, El Salvador, and Guatemala rose by 25 percent while migration from Mexico declined.[6] The USCCB's response to migration reflects these demographic trends, with much of their effort focused on the issues associated with the US-Mexico border and the migration flows from Central and South America.

In 2003, the USCCB collaborated with the Catholic bishops of Mexico to write a joint pastoral letter, *Strangers No Longer: Together on a Journey of Hope* (*SNL*). The letter builds on a history of CST on immigration, emphasizing the demands of the common good and the dignity of individuals and families as criteria for evaluating the reality of immigration. This letter is notable for its message as well as its collaborative development. The USCCB and the Mexican Conference of Catholic Bishops, who lead the Catholic Church in two nations whose perspectives on migration are grounded in different contexts, jointly declared that immigration is not just about

---

4. To learn more about the tensions experienced by early Catholic immigrants to the United States, see Jay Dolan, *In Search of an American Catholicism: A History of Religion and Culture in Tension* (Oxford: Oxford University Press, 2002).

5. Gustavo López and Kristen Bialik, "Key Findings About U.S. Immigrants," Pew Research Center (May 3, 2017).

6. D'Vera Cohn, Jeffrey S. Passel, and Ana Gonzalez-Barrera, "Rise in U.S. Immigrants From El Salvador, Guatemala and Honduras Outpaces Growth From Elsewhere," Pew Research Center (December 7, 2017).

national identity or affiliation. By working together to address the issue of migration, the bishops from both countries modeled the solidarity for which the Church has consistently advocated in debates on immigration. In their joint letter, the US and Mexican bishops promote solidarity by issuing pastoral directives that will help people in both countries respond to the situation of migrants and develop public policy directives that can help governments respond justly to the reality of migration. The principles of CST, especially the call to family, community, and participation, inform the bishops' pastoral directives and policy recommendations.

The bishops' letter identifies challenges and dangers that migrants often face—economic hardship at home, unsafe passage to their destination, and lack of protection where they settle—and notes that, as a result, migrants often find themselves in unstable or dangerous situations without the assistance they need. This is especially true for undocumented migrants afraid to seek assistance or legal protection for fear that they will be detained or deported. Many undocumented migrants seek refuge in religious organizations because they are afraid of the state.[7] Churches and faith-based organizations are thus in a unique position to establish trust among migrants and are able to provide them with resources regardless of their legal status.

The bishops of the United States and Mexico recognize the position of religious organizations, including the Catholic Church, to serve immigrants in need of help and commit themselves to their pastoral care, inviting local churches to always reveal a "spirit of hospitality" toward migrants (*SNL*, no. 42). Offering hospitality involves overcoming xenophobia and hostility toward migrants, and providing resources that they need to adjust to a new culture and achieve social stability. Church leaders, in particular, should undertake the task of "the building of structures of solidarity to accompany the migrant" (*SNL*, no. 40). The bishops stress that the Christian faith mandates welcoming the migrant, asking people to see Christ in the face of the stranger and the outcast: "For I was hungry and you gave me food, I was thirsty and you gave me drink, a stranger and you welcomed me" (Matthew 25:35). Within this theological framework, responding

---

7. Margarita Mooney, "The Catholic Bishops Conferences of the United States and France: Engaging Immigration as a Public Issue," *American Behavioral Scientist* 49:11 (July 2006): 1455–70.

to the migrant is part of the Church's ongoing task of conversion toward Christ. The bishops describe the implications of this in *SNL*.

> Part of the process of conversion of mind and heart deals with confronting attitudes of cultural superiority, indifference, and racism; accepting migrants not as foreboding aliens, terrorists, or economic threats, but rather as persons with dignity and rights, revealing the presence of Christ; and recognizing migrants as bearers of deep cultural values and rich faith traditions. (*SNL*, no. 40)

Catholic Social Teaching on Migration Rights

CST has insisted on the right to migrate since Pope Pius XII's *Exsul familia Nazarethana* (*The Exiled Family from Nazareth*, 1952). The Catholic Church's teaching, however, has also called for the investigation of the root causes of migration and the creation of conditions that will eliminate migration that is forced by economic hardship. CST has consistently challenged unrestricted liberal capitalism that exacerbates the gap between wealthy and poor nations. In *Populorum progressio* (*The Development of Peoples,* 1967) Pope Paul VI criticized a type of tyranny that results when profits and free competition are the guiding norms of economics (no. 26). The disparity of wealth among nations, supported by unfair trade agreements that favor wealthier nations and multinational corporations, creates the conditions in which citizens of less-developed countries, desperate to gain financial security, often feel compelled by necessity to migrate. Critiquing this reality, the US and Mexican bishops suggest that "this is the ideal situation for which the world and both countries should strive: one in which migration flows are driven by choice, not necessity" (*SNL*, no. 59).

The Church calls people to see the migrant first and foremost as a person with the same dignity and rights as all others and to serve the needs of immigrants without legal status-based discrimination.

Many migrants have chosen to leave family members behind in order to come to the United States to work and send money home because of extreme economic necessity or threat of violence. In 2016 immigrants sent an estimated $429 billion US dollars to family in their countries of origin.[8] This money supports international development when wealthier countries fail to provide such funds through international aid or enact unjust trade policies that disadvantage impoverished countries. Ultimately, the lack of international solidarity perpetuates economically driven migration and leads to the separation of families. This is problematic in light of the principle of the call to family, community, and participation because it ignores the demands of the global common good, and it undermines the basic social structure of the family. The reunification of families is a top priority for the bishops of the United States and Mexico. They critique immigration policies that weaken family unity and argue that the situation encourages undocumented immigration. The bishops argue that "a new framework must be established that will give Mexican families more opportunities to legally reunite with their loved ones in the United States" (SNL, no. 66).

The same economic forces that motivate migrants to leave their families in Mexico provide jobs in the United States. The reality is that immigrants (documented and undocumented) respond to a high demand in the US job market, working in jobs that many Americans do not want. Immigrants often work in construction, agriculture, and the service industry—traditionally, low-paying and labor-intensive jobs unsupported by unions. Furthermore, the demand of US consumers for cheap goods and services (especially when this demand is unmet by strong advocacy for labor) creates an economy that is dependent on low-wage workers.

The bishops, among others, argue that because the US economy has created the demand for migrant labor, it needs to make provisions for safe and fair participation in the economy. The bishops state, "the United States needs Mexican laborers to maintain a healthy economy and should make a special effort to provide legal avenues for Mexican workers to obtain in the United States jobs that provide a living wage and appropriate benefits and labor protections" (SNL, no.

---

8. World Bank, "Trends in Migration and Remittances 2017" (April 21, 2017), available at *http://www.worldbank.org/en/news/infographic/2017/04/21/trends-in-migration-and-remittances-2017.*

72). The bishops continue the Catholic social tradition's insistence on the rights of workers, which is grounded in the dignity of the human person and the dignity of work. These rights, which include a just wage, safe working conditions, and nondiscrimination in the workplace, transcend the legal status of an individual. The bishops defend the dignity of documented and undocumented workers while advocating for pathways to legalization of migrant workers in the United States. They state, "We recognize that, as an alternative to undocumented migration, an efficient legal pathway must be established that protects the basic labor rights of foreign-born workers" (*SNL*, no. 75). Specifically, they suggest that the United States needs to provide a greater number of both temporary and permanent worker visas to prevent the abuse of undocumented migrant workers (*SNL*, no. 72).

The principle of human dignity is at the heart of the bishops' response to migration. The bishops echo Pope John Paul II's unconditional defense of the dignity of the migrant. In his address on World Migration Day, he stated that "his [the migrant's] irregular legal status cannot allow the migrant to lose his dignity, since he is endowed with inalienable rights."[9] In other words, human rights must be protected regardless of one's legal status. This does not mean that the Catholic Church supports illegal immigration. In fact, the Catholic social tradition explicitly supports the right and responsibility of a nation to control its borders. However, the way that it controls its borders cannot violate the dignity of each person or disregard the global common good. *Strangers No Longer* states,

> The Catholic Church recognizes the right and responsibility of sovereign nations to control their borders and to ensure the security interests of their citizens. Therefore, we accept the legitimate role of the U.S. and Mexican governments in intercepting undocumented migrants who attempt to travel through or cross into one of the two countries. We do not accept, however, some of the policies and tactics that our governments have employed to meet this shared responsibility. (no. 78)

---

9. John Paul II, "Undocumented Migrants," no. 2, 1996 World Migration Day Address, available at *http://www.vatican.va/holy_father/john_paul_ii/messages/migration /documents/hf_jp-ii_mes_25071995_undocumented_migrants_en.html*.

Pope Francis's Solidarity with Migrants

Pope Francis greets the crowd during his 2013 visit to Lampedusa, Italy, where he celebrated Mass and called for solidarity with migrants.

Pope Francis has modeled the Catholic Church's solidarity with migrants since the beginning of his papacy. In 2013, during his first trip outside of Rome as pope, Francis visited Lampedusa, a small Italian island that serves as a major point of entry for African and Middle Eastern migrants seeking economic and political security in the European Union. There, Pope Francis prayed for the thousands of migrants who have died in the process of seeking a better life, and he called on the international community to overcome a "globalization of indifference." Continuing his advocacy for migrants and refugees, in 2015 Francis invited each parish in Europe to house a family fleeing the longstanding conflict in Syria. In *Evangelii gaudium* (*The Light of Faith,* 2013), Francis names migrants, refugees, and trafficked persons among the vulnerable for whom is he particularly concerned (*EG,* 210).

Using the principle of human dignity, the bishops critique some of the tactics practiced in the detainment centers on the US–Mexico border. The bishops offer examples of inhumane treatment, citing "documented abuses of migrants," the use of "excessive force" to detain migrants, and the use of "dilapidated detention facilities" to contain unaccompanied minors (*SNL*, nos. 80–82). The border initiatives employed to deter illegal immigration have proved to be largely ineffective, only driving migrants to pursue dangerous routes, as in the case of the popular Sonora Desert route. The number of migrant deaths doubled between 1994 and 2006 when the United States began enforcing more stringent border patrol at known crossing points.[10] In 2017, nearly three hundred migrants died crossing the US-Mexico border.[11] Drawing on the principle of human dignity, the bishops issue a defense of the sanctity of life and challenge the United States and Mexico to control their borders in a way that minimizes death and assists "migrants in distress" (*SNL*, no. 89).

The Kino Border Initiative

A number of religious and nonreligious organizations have responded to the need for humanitarian relief at the US-Mexico border. For example, the Kino Border Initiative (KBI) brings together the resources of the Catholic community to minister to migrants on both sides of the US-Mexico border. Sponsored by the California Province of Jesuits, the Catholic Diocese of Tucson, the Mexico Province of Jesuits, the Missionary Sisters of the Eucharist, the Jesuit Refugee Service/USA, and the Archdiocese of Hermosillo, KBI coordinates services near the border for recently deported migrants. The services include the provision of meals, first aid, and shelter. KBI also promotes education about

continued

10. US Government Accountability Office, "Illegal Immigration: Border Crossing Deaths Have Doubled Since 1995; Border Patrol's Efforts to Prevent Deaths Have Not Been Fully Evaluated," GAO-06-770 (Washington, DC: US Government Accountability Office, August 2006), 16; as cited in Donald Kerwin, "Rights, the Common Good, and Sovereignty in Service of the Human Person," in Donald Kerwin and Jill Marie Gerschutz, *And You Welcomed Me* (Lanham, MD: Lexington Press, 2009), 113.

11. United States Customs and Border Protection Sector Profile Fiscal Year 2017, available at *https://www.cbp.gov/sites/default/files/assets/documents/2017-Dec/USBP%20Stats%20FY2017%20sector%20profile.pdf*.

The Kino Border Initiative *continued*

migration by sponsoring immersion programs for high school and university students, allowing them to observe the reality of migration at the border. By focusing on collaboration among parishes on both sides of the US-Mexico border, KBI promotes solidarity and provides a visible expression of the Christian discipleship transcending national borders to defend human dignity and enhance the common good. See website: *https://www.kinoborder initiative.org/.*

Reading the Signs of the Times: Undocumented Immigrants in the United States

The context of migration is always shifting, making ongoing social analysis necessary. Because immigration is such an important political topic in the United States today, one is challenged continually to evaluate policies and proposals for immigration reform. This section will illustrate a small piece of a much larger and complex reality, focusing on the issue of undocumented immigrant youth and workers in the United States today. By highlighting the strong economic factors driving migration to the United States and briefly outlining the limited pathways to legal migration, this section sets up an ethical dilemma. Describing the work of Catholic theologian Daniel Groody on the topic demonstrates how the Catholic social tradition can inform the issue of migration.

On February 10, 2017, Daniel Ramirez Medina was detained by US Immigration and Customs Enforcement (ICE) agents and taken to an immigrant detention center in Tacoma, Washington, where he was held for more than a month. The 23-year-old man's detention resulted in public outcry and a lawsuit against the US Department of Homeland Security.

Medina had been approved to reside and work in the United States under the Deferred Action for Childhood Arrivals (DACA) program. Signed into law by an executive order by President Obama in 2012 and rescinded by President Trump in 2017, DACA protected certain undocumented immigrants from deportation. Medina, whose parents brought him to the United States from Mexico when he was seven years old, qualified for DACA because he met certain conditions—he was under age 16 when he arrived in the United States, he did not have a criminal record, and he was reported to be continuing his education. Although many "Dreamers" like Medina have lived in the United States most of their lives, their futures are shaped by changes in US immigration policies and enforcement practices.[12]

Medina wrote that his parents brought him to the United States to give him "a good shot at life."[13] A 2016 United Nations Human Development Report reveals a strong connection between migration and the pursuit of opportunities to develop as people and improve life for their families. The report indicates that the majority of international migrants travel from an underdeveloped country to a more economically developed country.[14] Mexico, the country of origin for most of the US foreign-born population, has a per capita Gross National Income rate of $9,040 as compared to the US $56,180.[15] The growing economic disparity between wealthy and poor nations undoubtedly fuels increased migration. Today, almost half of the world's population lives on less than two US dollars a day, and around 550 million people live on less than one US dollar per day.[16] This reality makes US wages attractive, even if workers are making less than the 2017 legal minimum of $7.25 per hour. Examining the reality of immigration in light of the global economy highlights the connection between human development and migration flows.

12. Daniel Ramirez Medina: "I'm a 'Dreamer,' but Immigration Agents Detained Me Anyway," in *The Washington Post* (March 13, 2017), available at *https://www.washingtonpost.com/posteverything/wp/2017/03/13/im-a-dreamer-immigration-agents-detained-me-anyway/?utm_term=.26f75b0d74e3*.

13. Ibid.

14. UN Human Development Report 2016, available at *http://hdr.undp.org/sites/default/files/2016_human_development_report.pdf*.

10. Data on GNI provided by the World Bank, available at *http://data.worldbank.org/indicator/NY.GNP.PCAP.CD*.

15. Data on 2016 GNI provided by the World Bank, available at *http://data.worldbank.org/indicator/NY.GNP.PCAP.CD*.

16. Global Commission on International Migration 2005 Report, 11.

Opportunities for people to migrate to the United States and work legally are limited.[17] The US Department of Homeland Security lists four broad categories designating pathways for non-US citizens to achieve legal permanent resident (LPR) status: (1) family-sponsorship preference (which includes children, spouses, and parents of US citizens), (2) employer-based sponsorship preference, (3) refugees and asylees preference, and (4) diversity preference (allowing immigrants of countries that have low migration flows to the United States).[18] Employer-based preferences are highly sought after but limited in number, accounting for only 13.7 percent of the LPRs in 2015.[19] Out of that percentage, the majority were professionals with an advanced degree or skilled workers in a sector identified as a priority area for the US economy.[20]

The majority of undocumented workers seeking permanent resident status in the United States work in sectors such as agricultural and domestic work, which do not require a college degree. Although the data show how difficult it is for these individuals to obtain legal status, they fulfill a strong demand in the US job market. The US immigration policy, however, does not reflect this economic reality, offering the majority of employer-based preferences to highly educated professionals with specialized skills. The US bishops have repeatedly advocated for comprehensive immigration reform that reflects this economic reality and prioritizes family unity.[21] US lawyers John Hoeffner and Michele Pistone conclude that "in particular, a discrepancy exists between the strength of forces propelling

---

17. Since 2016, it has become increasingly difficult to pursue legal migration to the United States. Through a series of executive orders, the Trump administration has implemented heightened screening and vetting of visa applicants, decreased the ceiling for refugee resettlement in the United States, issued a travel ban for citizens of certain Muslim-majority countries, and ordered the construction of a wall on the US-Mexico border.

18. US Department of Homeland Security 2015 Report on US Legal Permanent Residents, available at *https://www.dhs.gov/sites/default/files/publications/Lawful_Permanent_Residents_2015.pdf*.

19. Ibid.

20. Ibid.

21. US Conference of Catholic Bishops Office of Migration Policy and Public Affairs statement, "Catholic Church's Position on Immigration Reform" (August 2013), available at *http://www.usccb.org/issues-and-action/human-life-and-dignity/immigration/churchteachingonimmigrationreform.cfm*.

migrants into the United States and the ability of current law to recognize in some official way the reality of their presence. Hence, the problem of the undocumented immigrant."[22]

The problem of the undocumented immigrant can be examined from the perspectives of many different people—politicians, immigration lawyers, business owners and employees, and the millions who pursue international migration each year.[23] Catholic priest and scholar Daniel Groody examines migration from a theological perspective, emphasizing the Christian belief that the human person reflects the image and likeness of God. On this basis, he challenges some of the language used to categorize migrants such as *aliens* and *illegal*. Such language can obscure the humanity of migrants and promote attitudes and policies that undermine their human rights. Furthermore, categories fail to identify adequately the economic injustices motivating migration flows. Groody suggests that "categories such as legality and illegality, the documented and the undocumented, and citizen and alien, not only fail to come to terms with a new global reality, but they also leave gaping areas of injustice in their wake."[24] Emphasizing the humanity of migrants has moral implications, mandating policies that honor the rights of migrants and protect their dignity.

Summary and Integration for Service Learners

This chapter explored some ethical dimensions of migration with a focus on migration from Mexico to the United States. The Catholic Church has responded to the immediate needs of migrants, many of whom lack social and legal support. Recognizing the situation of these migrants, the USCCB and Mexican bishops have challenged local churches to be a place of refuge and help for migrants, providing

---

22. John Hoeffner and Michele Pistone, "But the Laborers Are Many: Catholic Social Teaching on Business, Labor, and Economic Migration." in Kerwin and Gerschutz, *And You Welcomed Me*, 69.

23. The UN estimates 244 million international migrants living abroad in 2015. See *http://www.un.org/sustainabledevelopment/blog/2016/01/244-million-international -migrants-living-abroad-worldwide-new-un-statistics-reveal*.

24. Daniel Groody, "Crossing the Divide: Foundations of a Theology of Migration and Refugees," *Theological Studies* 70 (2000): 639.

hospitality and assistance. The Catholic Church in the United States has also engaged in advocacy for just immigration reform guided by the priorities of protecting the rights and dignity of migrants. Their advocacy also focuses on promoting economic justice that allows everyone to participate in the international common good and on defending the unity of the family.

These guidelines are rooted in the Christian theological tradition, which insists that people are social beings, created in the image of a relational God and created for community with others. The call to family, community, and participation is rooted in this theology and has developed as a foundational principle of CST. The issues surrounding migration highlight the importance of this principle as it challenges people to promote solidarity in the international community, create pathways for participation in society among the marginalized, and protect the dignity of the family.

Having learned about some ethical dimensions of migration, revisit your responses to the questions in the introduction. Has the chapter led you to rethink any of your answers? Has it confirmed any of your assumptions about the meaning of community or the importance of family? How does the principle of the call to family, community, and participation inform your attitudes about migrants? Use the following vignette and questions to practice the see-judge-act process in relation to this topic.

See, Judge, Act in the Community

Vignette

Mary works in a leadership role at a Catholic parish that declared itself a sanctuary in January 2017 in response to executive orders that increased fear and uncertainty among immigrant communities. Since then, the parish has hosted "know your rights" trainings for the community and participates in the area's Rapid Response Network to be present to immigrant communities during US Immigration and Customs Enforcement (ICE) raids. In response to its declaration of sanctuary, the parish has received more requests for assistance than it can address.

The parish is currently accompanying Ana, a single mother with five children who migrated from Mexico earlier that year. After navigating the city's shelter system for several weeks, one of the children had a health crisis and was taken to the emergency room. When the family returned to the shelter where they were staying late that night, there were no beds and they slept on the streets. Mary is now working with other parishioners and community partners to help the family find stable housing. The parish also connected Ana to an immigration attorney who is assisting her with the lengthy process of filing for domestic violence-based asylum in the United States.

See: Social Analysis

- What social, political, and economic factors may have contributed to the woman's decision to seek asylum? Can you identify any social injustices that may have led to her migration?
- Consider the obstacles preventing the woman from finding stable housing for her family. How many of these factors could be attributed to her decisions? What factors may be beyond her control?

Judge: Ethical Reflection

- Consider the woman's situation in light of the principle of the call to family and community. What priorities emerge? When you consider the implications of this principle, do you see the woman's situation differently?
- Evaluate Groody's challenge to some of the language used to categorize migrants in light of CST. Can you identify language that better reflects the migrants' dignity and actual situation?

Act: Promoting Justice

- Based on what you have learned about CST and some of the challenges surrounding migration in the United States today, what do you think should be done to address the issue of undocumented migration?
- Identify immediate and long-term actions aligned with CST that respond to the situation of undocumented immigrants. What is the role of faith communities, nonprofit organizations, and the government in taking these actions?

Suggestions for Further Social Analysis in a Service-Learning Context

- What services are available for immigrants in a selected city or service-learning context? How are these services promoted and accessed? What services can immigrants obtain without documentation?
- Research data on migration flows into a selected city, and identify any patterns. What political and economic factors in host countries and in the selected city might be motivating these migration patterns?
- Research the immigration enforcement policies and practices of a selected state. How do these relate to federal policies? What are some of the current debates behind state and federal policies?

For Further Study on Catholic Social Thought and Migration

Print Materials

Collier, Elizabeth and Charles Strain with Catholic Relief Services. *Global Migration: What's Happening, Why, and a Just Response.* Winona, MN: Anselm Academic, 2017.

Cruz, Gemma Tulud. "Toward an Ethic of Risk: Catholic Social Teaching and Immigration Reform." *Studies in Christian Ethics* 24, no. 3 (August 2011): 294–310.

De la Torre, Miguel. *Trials of Hope and Terror: Testimonies on Immigration.* Maryknoll, NY: Orbis Press, 2009.

Groody, Daniel. *A Promised Land, a Perilous Journey: Theological Perspectives on Migration.* Notre Dame, IN: University of Notre Dame Press, 2008.

Heyer, Kristin. *Kinship across Borders: A Christian Ethic of Migration.* Washington, DC: Georgetown University Press, 2012.

Kerwin, Donald, and Jill Marie Gerschutz. *And You Welcomed Me: Migration and Catholic Social Teaching.* Lanham, MD: Lexington Books, 2009.

Websites

Catholic Relief Services University, "I am Migration," *http://university .crs.org/migration.*

Offers resources to learn about migration and reflect on it through the lens of Catholic teaching. Ideas for action and advocacy are included.

Jesuit Refugee Services, *http://jrsusa.org/.*

Provides recommended reading and highlights current news related to refugees. The mission of JRS is to accompany, serve, and advocate for refugees.

Justice for Immigrants, *https://justiceforimmigrants.org/.*

A project of the US Conference of Catholic Bishops to educate about immigration in the United States and advocate for comprehensive immigration reform in line with Catholic social thought.

Justice for Workers and the Dignity of Work

Introduction

Protecting the dignity of work and justice for workers is a fundamental principle of Catholic social teaching (CST). The topic of work is prominent in many of the major social encyclicals, including Pope Leo XIII's *Rerum novarum* (*On the Condition of Labor*, 1891), which addressed the ethical dimensions of work in the context of the Industrial Revolution, and has continued to be an important theme in CST. Reflect on your understanding of the meaning of work and its moral dimensions using the following questions:

- What is the meaning and purpose of work? Does your understanding of work include unpaid work? Does it include service learning?

- What is your experience of work? Have any of your work experiences raised justice-related concerns? If so, explain. What are your hopes for work in the future? What, if anything, might stand in the way of you realizing your hopes?

- How do you understand the Catholic Church's call to protect the dignity of work? How is the dignity of work realized? What signs might indicate that the dignity of work is not being protected?

The unjust treatment of workers signals that a community is failing to protect the dignity of work. Signs of injustice can take on many forms, including long-term unemployment, insufficient wages, and exploitation in the workplace. Consider what you already know about the violation of workers' rights.

- What rights do workers have? Who is responsible for enforcing rules that protect these rights?
- Is work a concern among people you may have met in a service-learning context? If so, what are their concerns? How do these people's hopes about work compare with your hopes for work?
- What conditions, practices, and policies create security for workers? What conditions, practices, and policies make workers vulnerable?

This chapter will address the topic of work by highlighting major developments in CST on the dignity of work and rights of workers. It will examine teachings about work in the early social encyclicals, focusing on *Rerum novarum,* highlight the connection between work and integral human development in the writings of Pope Paul VI, and review John Paul II's personalist approach to work in *Laborem exercens (On Human Work,* 1981). Then the chapter will examine some ways the United States Conference of Catholic Bishops (USCCB) have applied the principle of the dignity of work to labor issues in the United States. Next, the chapter will present information that can inform social analysis about vulnerable workers in the United States today. The final section of the chapter provides a summary followed by a service-learning vignette and a series of questions designed to help readers practice aspects of the see-judge-act process.

The Dignity of Work in Catholic Social Teaching

Labor in the Early Social Encyclicals

The first social encyclical, *Rerum novarum (On the Condition of Labor),* focuses on ethical questions raised in the aftermath of the Industrial Revolution, which began in Europe in the late eighteenth century and later spread to other countries including the United States. The nature and context of work had shifted significantly with new forms of production that supported the economic system of capitalism. Factories were able to manufacture a surplus of goods, and owners of raw materials employed workers to turn those materials into products. However, without the government regulations that many people rely on today to ensure that workers are treated with fairness and dignity, employers could legally exploit workers in order to maximize profits. As a result, industrial workers endured long hours, often without breaks or weekends, and they often worked in unhealthy or dangerous conditions for poor wages. This new situation raised questions about the treatment of workers and the conditions of their work.

In *Rerum novarum*, Pope Leo XIII denounced the competitive and individualistic spirit of capitalism that drove employers to exploit workers, and he rejected the utopian vision of equality that socialists offered as an alternative to capitalism. The pope argued that natural inequalities necessarily exist in social life and that people should treat each other with dignity but not expect that inequalities be leveled (*RN*, no. 17). Against the socialists, Leo XIII defended the worker's natural right to private property and rejected intervention from the state that would violate this right. At the same time, the pope argued that the state has a role in protecting the natural rights of workers, such as the right to private property and the right to wages that are sufficient for supporting a family (*RN*, nos. 30–34). This understanding of the government's role in economic life is at the core of the Catholic Church's current support of living wage laws and labor regulations.

Leo XIII was also concerned that socialists would undermine the moral authority of the Catholic Church. The pope did not want to lose the working class to the promise of hope the socialists offered workers. In *Rerum novarum*, Leo XIII invites people to look to the Catholic Church and the Christian faith for meaning in their suffering. Thus, he offers a theological interpretation of the suffering associated with work, suggesting that it is a result of the fall recounted in the book of Genesis (3:17–19). Leo XIII suggests,

> As regards bodily labor, even had man never fallen from the state of innocence, he would not have remained wholly idle; but that which would then have been his free choice and his delight became afterwards compulsory, and the painful

expiation for his disobedience. "Cursed be the earth in thy work; in thy labor thou shalt eat of it all the days of thy life." (*RN*, no. 17)

Minimum Wage vs. Living Wage

Catholic social thought advocates for a living wage because minimum wage laws do not necessarily prevent families from living in poverty. Based on the 2017 federal minimum wage of $7.25 per hour, a full-time worker earns about $15,000 per year.[1] The 2016 US Census Bureau data report identifies the poverty threshold for a family consisting of two adults and one child at $16,543.[2] Households headed by single mothers are particularly vulnerable to poverty, with the gender pay gap being one contributing factor. In 2015 women on average earned 80 percent of the earnings of their male counterparts.[3]

The principle behind the argument for a living wage is that people who are earning wages for full-time employment should not have to live in poverty. Living wages are based on estimates of the cost of living in particular areas. The state of California, for example, had a minimum wage of $10.00 per hour in 2017, but experts estimated that the living wage for a family of two adults and one child in California at that time was $26.46 per hour.[4]

Pope Leo XIII connects the suffering of workers to human sinfulness. Subsequent developments of CST point out two time-bound limitations of Leo XIII's understanding of work. First, locating the

---

1. Kai Filion, "Minimum Wage Anniversary: Still Helping Millions of Workers Get By, but Just Barely," Economic Policy Institute (July 23, 2010), available at *http://www.epi.org/publication/minimum_wage_anniversary_still_helping_millions_of_workers_get_by_but_/*.

2. The United States Census Bureau, "Income and Poverty in the United States: 2016," available at *https://www.census.gov/library/publications/2017/demo/p60-259.html*.

3. United States Census Bureau, "Income and Poverty in the United States: 2015," available at *https://www.census.gov/library/publications/2016/demo/p60-256.html*.

4. According to the Massachusetts Institute of Technology (MIT) Living Wage Calculator, available at *http://livingwage.mit.edu*.

suffering of human labor in the fall does not promote a structural analysis of economic injustices that perpetuate the suffering of workers. Second, it does not capture the positive aspect of work as an expression of human subjectivity. By focusing on the person doing the work rather than the work itself, work can be understood as the way that people express themselves as individuals and participate in the social life of a community.

The Catholic social tradition is marked by continuity with and development of Leo XIII's thoughts on labor. The tradition has consistently supported the dignity of work, the provision of a living wage so the worker can support a family and maintain private property, and the value of labor unions in protecting the rights of workers and promoting cooperation in the labor market. Two developments since *Rerum novarum* are particularly notable. First, Pope Paul VI's approach to integral human development, which locates the aspiration for freedom and equality in the nature of the human person, challenged Leo XIII's assumption that natural inequalities exist. Second, John Paul II's development of a personalist approach to work, which emphasized the positive value of work as an expression of the individual and the way that an individual participates in community, nuanced Leo XIII's linking of work and suffering as part of the lot of fallen humanity.

Pope Paul VI: Human Development and Work

During the Second Vatican Council, Pope Paul VI attended to developing countries and human development. At this time the United Nations was raising awareness about the effects of colonization and global inequalities.[5] Paul VI also wanted to raise awareness about the shocking disparity between rich and poor countries. His focus, however, went beyond the rich and poor disparity to include what he described as integral human development. Two years after the close of the council, Paul VI wrote his encyclical letter *Populorum progressio* (*The Development of Peoples*, 1967). In *Populorum progressio* (*PP*), the pope described human development as follows:

---

5. Marvin Mich, *Catholic Social Teaching and Movements* (Mystic, CT: Twenty-Third Publications, 2006), 155–57.

The development we speak of here cannot be restricted to economic growth alone. To be authentic, it must be well rounded; it must foster the development of each man and of the whole man. . . . Self-development, however, is not left up to man's option. Just as the whole of creation is ordered toward its Creator, so too the rational creature should of his own accord direct his life to God, the first truth and the highest good. Thus human self-fulfillment may be said to sum up our obligations. Moreover, this harmonious integration of our human nature, carried through by personal effort and responsible activity, is destined for a higher state of perfection. United with the life-giving Christ, man's life is newly enhanced; it acquires a transcendent humanism which surpasses its nature and bestows new fullness of life. This is the highest goal of human self-fulfillment. (nos. 14, 16)

In Paul VI's view, the aspiration to the fullness of life is an innate part of the human person, an expression of one's dignity and willed by God. Social structures that thwart the human drive toward conditions that support the fullness of life can lead to social conflict and even violent revolution (*PP*, no. 30). By acknowledging the possibility of violence, Paul VI is not condoning revolutionary violence, but he is expressing more sympathy toward revolutionary movements than Leo XIII did in 1891. Paul VI follows his immediate predecessor, Pope John XXIII, in affirming that justice and the protection of human rights are the foundations of peace. This perspective is grounded in the observation that social inequalities inhibit lasting peace. Paul VI's emphasis on integral human development and the transformation of unjust structures challenges the notion that natural inequalities exist. His perspective locates injustices in the dynamics of human history rather than unchanging features of human nature. The thought of Paul VI lays the foundation for workers to expect justice so that they can, through their work, achieve self-fulfillment.

Pope John Paul II: A Personalist Approach to Labor

On the ninetieth anniversary of *Rerum novarum* (*On the Condition of Labor*), Pope John Paul II issued a social encyclical on human work, *Laborem exercens* (*On Human Work*). Many people consider this encyclical to be one of the greatest contributions to the Catholic Church's social teaching on work. [6] It exemplifies John Paul II's personalist worldview, which locates the human person at the center of reality and judges reality based on how it conforms to the conviction that all people have inherent dignity. Within a personalist perspective, the human person must never be a marginal concern but is rather the central concern of decisions and actions.[7] Personalism stresses that the human person must never be an object, something to be acted on, but must always be the subject of social life, with agency, dignity, and freedom.

By rejecting all thought and action that objectifies people, personalism adds an important dimension to the Catholic Church's understanding of work. The *Compendium of the Social Doctrine of the Church* (2004) summarizes this dimension by saying that "*all of social life is an expression of its unmistakable protagonist: the human person*" (no. 106).[8] In other words, people are the center of social life, the main characters in history as it unfolds. The specifically Christian understanding of personalism, which John Paul II developed, views and evaluates reality through the lens of a theological understanding of the human person: the human person is created in the image and likeness of God, redeemed by God, and destined for union with God at the end of time.

This perspective shapes John Paul II's understanding of work in several ways. First, he insists in *Laborem exercens* (*LE*) that the human person is and must always be treated as the subject of work.

---

6. On the reactions to *Laborem exercens*, see Patricia Lamoureux, "Commentary on *Laborem exercens* (On Human Work)," in *Modern Catholic Social Teaching: Commentaries and Interpretations*, ed. Kenneth Himes, et al. (Washington, DC: Georgetown University Press, 2005), 408–10.

7. Bernard Brady, *Essential Catholic Social Thought* (Maryknoll, NY: Orbis, 2008), 32–36.

8. Pontifical Council for Justice and Peace, *The Compendium of the Social Doctrine of the Church* (Libreria Editrice Vaticana, 2004).

He states: "As *a person, man is therefore the subject of work*. As a person he works, he performs various actions belonging to the work process; independently of their objective content, these actions must all serve to realize his humanity, to fulfill the calling to be a person that is his by reason of his very humanity" (*LE*, no. 6). In other words, the value of the person is never determined by the kind of work he or she performs. The product of work can never be valued above the person and the person can never be considered alongside the other means of productivity. Within a personalist perspective on work, there is a fundamental difference between a person and a machine, a person and a material, a person and a profit. For the pope, the person must always be the primary concern and should never be treated as a means to an end.

John Paul II grounds work in the subjectivity of the human person by referring to the book of Genesis, which invites people to "fill the earth and subdue it" (1:28). He interprets this passage to mean that the impulse to work is grounded in and unique to human nature. This impulse is seen as God's invitation to participate in creation, contribute to social life, and express one's unique dignity. As such, work should not just be something that a person endures for the sake of survival. Even though many people have to work in jobs that they experience as obligatory and meaningless, the fundamental meaning of work is tied to the nature of the human person. Work is an expression of the human person: "Work is a good thing for man—a good thing for his humanity—because through work man *not only transforms nature*, adapting it to his own needs, but he also *achieves fulfillment* as a human being and indeed, in a sense, becomes 'more a human being'" (*LE*, no. 9).

John Paul II's personalist understanding of work highlights that work is a human activity with moral significance and a positive expression of the worker as a person. If one considers work to be an expression of human subjectivity, then work is personal. Considering the personal dimension of work can help one understand why people often express anger when someone takes credit for their work. It can also help explain why people can become depressed when they can no longer work. Work is also social. Work allows people to participate in their family, community, and the larger society. Within the framework offered by John Paul II, the way that individuals define their work, relate to workers, and structure their lives around work carries moral significance.

Pope Francis has also denounced the exploitation of workers in his rejection of economic policies that elevate profit over the well-being of the person. In a 2013 meeting with unemployed workers in Sardinia, Francis was quoted saying, "Not paying fairly, not giving a job because you are only looking at how to make a profit, that goes against God."[9] In 2014, Francis tweeted about the dignity of domestic workers—those who provide care for children, older adults, and people with disabilities—naming their work as a "precious service."[10] Finally, in his encyclical on integral ecology, Francis advocates for protecting employment, citing John Paul II's view that work is how we participate in the creative activity of God (*LS*, 124).

The United States Conference of Catholic Bishops on Labor

CST's call to defend the dignity of work and the rights of workers has practical implications for approaching work-related issues such as labor unions, wages, working conditions, and employment. The USCCB has applied CST to particular issues affecting US workers. This section will present a brief discussion of the role of Catholics in the early labor movement and an overview of the themes of the USCCB's recent Labor Day statements.

The Early Labor Movement

The early labor movement in the United States relied heavily on Catholic participation. In the late 1800s and early 1900s, Catholic immigrants from Ireland, Italy, and Germany made up a large portion of the labor market. Like many immigrants today, the immigrants of that era tended to work in jobs that made them vulnerable to insufficient wages, unsafe working conditions, and long workdays. Labor unions developed to give workers a voice to advocate for fairness in the workplace.

---

9. John Coleman, "Pope Francis on the Dignity of Labor," *America* (November 20, 2013).

10. @ Pontifex (2:29 AM–29 Jul 2014) *https://twitter.com/pontifex/status/4940520 20127424513?lang=en.*

Lay Catholics were instrumental in the development of one of the first labor unions in the United States, the Knights of Labor, in 1869. Despite strong participation among laypeople, the Catholic hierarchy was divided over whether to support the Knights of Labor, largely because of internal debates within the Catholic Church on how the Church should express itself as a religious minority in a predominantly Protestant country. Some bishops argued that Catholics should participate in the public life of American society by sending their kids to public schools and interacting with non-Catholics. Others encouraged Catholics to support Catholic schools and avoid socializing with non-Catholics. The question at the heart of the debate was how to assimilate into American life and maintain Catholic identity, which was also tied to a cultural identity as immigrants.[11] "Some of the hierarchy opposed the Knights of Labor out of fear that labor unions promoted secrecy, anarchy, and socialism."[12] At stake in this debate was the pastoral question of how to serve a Catholic immigrant population that was working class and a religious minority in the United States. Also at stake was the question of how to interpret and apply the Church's emerging social teaching in a non-European context.

Though Catholics in Europe had different concerns than Catholics of the United States, many of the teachings in *Rerum novarum* were applicable in the United States, particularly its defense of the rights of workers. Ultimately, US Cardinal James Gibbons was able in 1887 to convince the Vatican officially to support the Knights of Labor by drawing on the Catholic Church's social teaching. He quoted *Rerum novarum* to convince the pope that labor unions had an important role in society by giving a voice to workers. This had lasting implications in the development of the Catholic social tradition in the United States. Catholic historian John O'Brien notes, "Once the Vatican lifted the ban on the Knights, the church was perceived as being officially on the side of labor."[13]

---

11. For a historical analysis of this period, see Jay Dolan, *The American Catholic Experience: A History from Colonial Times to the Present* (Notre Dame, IN: The University of Notre Dame Press, 1992).

12. John O'Brien, *George Higgins and the Quest for Worker Justice: The Evolution of Catholic Social Thought in America* (Lanham, MD: Rowman & Littlefield Publishers, 2005), 29–30.

13. Ibid., 32.

Labor Priests in the United States

The Catholic Church's support of labor was exemplified in the early 1900s by labor priests. Labor priests were leading advocates for the rights of workers, supporting strikes and boycotts and providing encouragement to workers using the principles of *Rerum novarum* (*On the Condition of Labor*).[14] For example, Peter Yorke, a Catholic priest from San Francisco, supported workers through his writings and activism. He helped organize strikes among dockworkers as well as cable car workers who were fighting for fair wages and reasonable work hours.[15]

John Ryan, a labor priest and scholar who influenced the US bishops, applied CST to labor issues in the United States. Ryan, a professor at the Catholic University of America, taught and wrote about economic justice in the aftermath of World War I. Specifically, he used CST to advocate for a living wage, federal and state laws designed to protect workers, and the development of labor unions to strengthen the decision-making power of workers.[16]

The US bishops officially addressed some labor and economic issues in the United States in their 1919 document, *Bishops' Program of Social Reconstruction*.[17] In this document the bishops echoed much of Ryan's thought, advocating for workers' right to organize and receive just wages from their employers. In addition, the bishops argued that the government is responsible for protecting the rights of workers. The *Program of Social Reconstruction* reflects a shift in the US Catholic bishops' stance on labor. Within a few decades, the bishops had gone from being divided on whether to support unions to supporting organized labor, living wages, child labor laws, and social welfare systems.[18]

---

14. Ibid., 40–56.

15. Ibid., 46.

16. Mary Elsbernd, "Work and Workers in the Pastoral Letters of the United States Conference of Bishops," *Louvain Studies* 19 (1994): 222–24.

17. *Bishops' Program of Social Reconstruction* [reprint], Washington, DC: National Catholic Welfare Conference, 1950.

18. For a historical account of this era, see Elsbernd, "Work and Workers."

The United States Conference of Catholic Bishops' Recent Labor Day Statements

Today, the USCCB continues to speak on labor and the economy. One way they do this is by issuing a "Labor Day Statement" each year that draws on the same principles of CST that influenced the early Catholic labor priests to address contemporary situations.

The 2009 Labor Day statement, for example, draws on Pope Benedict XVI's social encyclical, *Caritas in veritate* (*Charity in Truth*, 2009), which identifies work as an expression of workers' dignity and creativity, allowing them to reflect the image and likeness of God in the world. The statement points out an implication of this theological understanding of work, suggesting that the "vision of cooperation with God in building up this world through our work underscores the need for us all to cooperate and collaborate with one another in making work and the workplace a project of human solidarity and mutual respect."[19]

The 2010 and 2011 Labor Day statements focus on the issue of widespread unemployment and poverty in the context of an economic recession. In the 2011 statement, the bishops remind readers that these issues "are not just economic, but also ethical. They are not just institutional, but also personal."[20] Drawing on the social teaching of the Catholic Church, the bishops offer principles to guide ethical responses to the labor issues that pay particular attention to how these issues impact people. They emphasize the need to work together to alleviate unemployment and to promote policies that reflect a preferential option for the poor and vulnerable.

In the 2011 Labor Day statement, the bishops also discuss the Catholic Church's position on labor unions, stating,

---

19. Bishop William F. Murphy, Chairman of the Committee on Domestic Justice and Human Development, USCCB, "Labor Day Statement: The Value of Work; The Dignity of the Human Person" (September 7, 2009), available at *http://www.usccb.org /issues-and-action/human-life-and-dignity/labor-employment/upload/labor-day-2009.pdf.*

20. Bishop Stephen Blaire, Chairman of the Committee on Domestic Justice and Human Development, USCCB, "Labor Day Statement: Human Costs and Moral Challenges of a Broken Economy" (September 5, 2011), available at *http://www.usccb .org/about/domestic-social-development/upload/Labor-Day-2011.pdf.*

Beginning in *Rerum novarum*, the Church has consistently supported efforts of workers to join together to defend their rights and protect their dignity. . . . Without endorsing every tactic of unions or every outcome of collective bargaining, the Church affirms the rights of workers in public and private employment to choose to come together to form and join unions, to bargain collectively, and to have an effective voice in the workplace.[21]

The 2017 Labor Day statement connects worker justice to larger economic realities. Drawing upon the teachings of Pope Francis, the statement denounces a "throw-away culture" that elevates consumerism and sees labor as a means to an end. The bishops argue for laws to protect workers from wage theft and insufficient wages. They also advocate for laws that incentivize ethical entrepreneurship that honors the dignity of work. The bishops give special attention to vulnerable workers, echoing earlier support for unions as a means to give vulnerable workers a voice. "Unions are especially valuable when they speak on behalf of the poor, the immigrant, and the person returning from prison."[22]

The bishops' affirmation of CST's support of labor unions is significant in light of contemporary debates about the role of labor unions in the US economy. The strong Catholic support of labor unions in the early part of the twentieth century weakened as Catholics moved into the middle and upper classes in the second half of the twentieth century.[23] The bishops remind their audience that, even as contexts change, the Church's support of workers' rights, including the right to form unions, has been consistent.

---

21. Ibid.

22. Bishop Frank J. Dewane, Chairman of the Committee on Domestic Justice and Human Development, USCCB, "Labor Day Statement 2017," available at *http://www.usccb.org/issues-and-action/human-life-and-dignity/labor-employment/upload/Labor-Day-2017.pdf*.

23. Kristen Hannum, "Labor Pains," *US Catholic* 76, no. 8 (August 2011): 12–17. Hannum cites findings by the Pew Research Forum indicating that 48 percent of Catholics and 42 percent of Protestants view unions favorably.

Reading the Signs of the Times: Vulnerable Workers

This section will further consider the rights of workers by presenting information about vulnerable workers in the United States—information that contributes to the social analysis one might do when following the see-judge-act process to plan action that responds to work-related injustices.

In 2006 agricultural worker Maricruz Ladino reported that she was sexually harassed on multiple occasions and eventually assaulted by the man who supervised her work on a lettuce farm in Salinas, CA. She waited several months to report her supervisor out of fear she would lose her job. In fact, Ladino was fired after making a formal complaint against her supervisor. She responded by filing a civil suit against the company, who settled out of court in 2010.[24]

Ladino's story was featured in a 2013 documentary, *Rape in the Fields*. The documentary was produced by a team of investigative journalists after a year of interviewing women agricultural workers. The reporters documented numerous accounts of sexual harassment and assault, identifying a number of factors that contribute to the vulnerability of workers in this industry. Like Ladino, many of the women are migrants, some of whom lack documentation to work legally in the United States. These workers may remain silent about their abuse out of reasonable fear of deportation. Agricultural workers tend to earn low wages and face financial instability due to the seasonal nature of work and other factors. Without job security and financial stability, it is likely that workers feel powerless before their supervisors because they fear losing their jobs. The reporters conclude, "The combination of financial desperation and tenuous immigration status make agricultural workers vulnerable to workplace violence and less inclined to report crimes."[25]

---

24. Sasha Khokha, "Silenced by Status, Farmworkers Face Rape, Sexual Abuse," National Public Radio, All Things Considered (November 5, 2013), available at *http://www.npr.org/2013/11/05/243219199/silenced-by-status-farm-workers-face-rape-sexual-abuse*.

25. Bernice Yeung and Grace Rubenstein, The Center for Investigative Reporting, "Female Workers Face Rape, Harassment in U.S. Agriculture Industry," PBS Frontline Report (June 25, 2013), available at *http://www.pbs.org/wgbh/pages/frontline/social-issues/rape-in-the-fields/female-workers-face-rape-harassment-in-u-s-agriculture-industry/*.

Farmworkers in the United States are particularly at risk for exploitation due to the laws and the effects of immigration status. The federal Fair Labor Standards Act sets different policies for farmworkers than for other sectors of the workforce and does not address conditions unique to agricultural work.[26] Specifically, employers are not required to ensure safety from the heat, leaving farmworkers vulnerable to heat exhaustion and other heat-related health issues. Federal child labor laws aim to protect young workers, but the rules for the agricultural sector of the workforce do not provide the same protections as for other sectors. Children as young as twelve can do farm work as long as it is outside of school hours and their parents give consent.[27] The immigration status of many agricultural workers makes them more vulnerable to exploitation on the job as they are afraid to seek legal protection of their rights. The majority of agricultural jobs are held by people born outside of the United States, many of whom lack authorization to work legally in the United States.[28]

The Rights of Agricultural Workers

The USCCB addressed the ethical dimensions of agricultural work in their 2003 pastoral letter, *For I Was Hungry and You Gave Me Food: Catholic Reflections on Food, Farmers, and Farmworkers.* The bishops draw on the Catholic social tradition's framework for economic justice, stating, "We believe that the economy, including the agricultural economy, must serve people, not the other way around. . . . Employers are obligated to treat their workers with dignity, providing decent wages, safe working conditions, and humane living conditions."

---

26. The Fair Labor Standards Act (FLSA) regulates the minimum wage, youth employment, hours worked per week, and overtime within the United States. Many states have additional regulations for these categories. See the US Department of Labor's website at *http://www.dol.gov.*

27. See the Department of Labor's website at *http://www.dol.gov/whd/regs/compliance/childlabor102.pdf.*

28. United States Department of Agriculture Economic Research Service Farm Labor Statistics (updated September 27, 2016), available at *https://www.ers.usda.gov/topics/farm-economy/farm-labor/background.aspx#demographic.*

Cesar Chavez and Dolores Huerta

Cesar Chavez (1927–1993) and Dolores Huerta (1930–), Mexican American activists, and labor organizers established the United Farm Workers in 1962 to promote just working conditions and fair wages for people working in the agricultural sector of California. Huerta and Chavez advocated for nonviolent means of change, including boycotts, fasting, and public witness. Drawing upon Catholic social teaching, they defended the rights of workers and dignity of immigrants.

© William Warren / SuperStock

Cesar Chavez and Dolores Huerta at a hunger strike, one of the nonviolent strategies they employed to organize agricultural workers.

Day laborers—individuals hired on an informal basis mainly for construction work, home repairs, moving assistance, and gardening— represent another especially vulnerable population in the US labor market. The majority of day laborers are employed in some form of construction work, which reports a high rate of job-related injuries. The Bureau of Labor Statistics listed the construction industry as having the highest number of work-related fatalities in 2016.[29] The immigration status of the majority of day laborers may increase their risk of injury in the construction industry. A 2006 study reported that the majority of these workers are Latino immigrants and 75 percent are undocumented.[30] Without legal authorization to work, day

---

29. US Bureau of Labor Statistics, US Department of Labor (2016), available at *https://www.bls.gov/news.release/pdf/cfoi.pdf.*

30. Abel Valenzuela, Jr., Nik Theodore, Edwin Melendez, and Ana Luz Gonzalez, "On the Corner: Day Labor in the United States" (January 2006).

laborers often take the most dangerous jobs and are afraid to oppose unsafe conditions.[31]

Social ethicist Kristin Heyer identifies a number of injustices day laborers experience. These include wage-theft[32] and exposure to unsafe working conditions.[33] Heyer draws on CST to advocate for the protection of workers' rights regardless of their legal status. Catholic teaching grounds human rights, including the rights of workers, in human dignity, making them universal and intrinsic. Heyer applies this to the context of undocumented workers, arguing that "undocumented workers and would-be workers are entitled to basic safeguards in light of longstanding Catholic social teachings on human rights and the rights of workers."[34]

Summary and Integration for Service Learners

The dignity of work is a central principle of CST. This chapter highlighted the development of this principle from *Rerum novarum* (*On the Condition of Labor*) to the personalist understanding of work in *Laborem exercens* (*On Human Work*). The personalist understanding of work articulated by Pope John Paul II emphasizes the central importance of the person as the subject of work and grounds the Church's critique of structures that lead to treating people as objects without rights and freedom. As a subject, the worker must be recognized as valuable and worthy of respect. Exploring work as a topic for social ethics invites reflection on how work enhances or diminishes the dignity of the worker.

With this foundation in mind, the USCCB has advocated for the dignity of work and the rights of workers. Drawing on CST, they have advocated for the right to work, the right to receive

---

31. Ibid.

32. Wage theft refers to a number of ways that employers unlawfully withhold wages from a worker. Some examples include failing to pay overtime, making an employee work off the clock, and failing to pay the legal minimum wage. See Kim Bobo, *Wage Theft in America: Why Millions of Working Americans Are Not Getting Paid—And What We Can Do About It*, second edition (New York: New Press, 2011).

33. Kristin Heyer, "Strangers in Our Midst: Day Laborers and Just Immigration Reform," *Political Theology* 9, no. 4 (October 2008): 436.

34. Ibid., 426.

high enough wages to support oneself and one's family with dignity, and the right to working conditions that are worthy of the human person. US society today does not succeed in protecting these rights for all workers. Those employed in agriculture and as day laborers in construction are especially vulnerable to exploitation. Now that you have read about CST as it relates to work and information about the situation of some US workers, revisit your answers to the questions at the beginning of the chapter. Would you answer any questions differently? Use the following vignette and questions to practice aspects of the see-judge-act process in relation to this topic.

See, Judge, Act in the Community

Vignette

A service learner working in an inner-city technology laboratory teaches computer skills to low-income adults. During her time in the technology lab, the student met a middle-aged man named Daniel who had been unemployed for more than a year after a back injury forced him to leave his job harvesting produce at a nearby farm. The student discovered that Daniel did not have regular access to the Internet, making it nearly impossible for him to search for jobs online. Daniel was eligible for subsidized Internet service; however, the service was slow in his apartment and outages were frequent. At 57, he feels behind on his ability to use technology and worries that it is going to hold him back from finding a job even though he has years of work experience.

See: Social Analysis

- What are some of the factors that may be contributing to this man's long-term unemployment? Can you identify any possible injustices that may be factors?
- What are some possible background experiences that may have contributed to the student's access to reliable Internet service and the man's lack of access? Can you identify any possible injustices that may account for the difference between the student's ability to use technology and the unemployed man's lack of ability?

Judge: Ethical Reflection

- Consider the situation of the man in the vignette in light of CST's principles of human dignity and the dignity of work. How might the principles of CST challenge the man's previous employers? How might the principles help to guide the work of those aiming to serve the unemployed?
- What is the difference between viewing workers as objects versus viewing them as subjects as articulated in CST? Does this understanding influence how you perceive the man in the vignette?

Act: Promoting Justice

- What might be done to address both the immediate and long-term needs of vulnerable workers and the unemployed? What specific policies and practices might support these efforts?
- Identify actions aligned with CST's call for the protection of the rights of workers that respond to the situation of vulnerable agriculture workers. Who is responsible for protecting the rights of such workers?

Suggestions for Further Social Analysis in a Service-Learning Context

- Research the unemployment rate in a particular area of a selected city, perhaps an area where a service-learning setting you are familiar with is located. Compare this rate with rates for other areas of the city, the state, and the country.
- Learn about the wage and labor laws in a selected city. Investigate whether some sectors of the workforce are vulnerable to violations of these laws.
- Learn more about a selected service organization that works to protect the rights of vulnerable workers. What problems does it aim to solve, and what resources, programs, and services does it provide?

For Further Study on Catholic Social Thought and Workers' Rights

Printed Materials

Beyer, Gerald. "Advocating Worker Justice: A Catholic Ethicist's Toolkit." *Journal of Religious Ethics* 45, no. 2 (2017): 226–50.

Bobo, Kim. "Do Catholics Still Care about Labor?" *America* 193, no. 5 (August 29, 2005): 10–13.

Finn, Daniel. "Human Work and Catholic Social Thought." *American Journal of Economics and Sociology* 71, no. 4 (October 2012): 874–85.

Heyer, Kristin E. "Strangers in Our Midst: Day Laborers and Just Immigration Reform." *Political Theology* 9, no. 4 (October 2008): 425–53.

O'Brien, John. *George G. Higgins and the Quest for Worker Justice: The Evolution of Catholic Social Thought in America.* Lanham, MD: Sheed & Ward, 2004.

Prouty, Marco G. *Cesar Chavez, the Catholic Bishops, and the Farmworkers' Struggle for Justice.* Tucson, AZ: University of Arizona Press, 2006.

Websites

Catholic Scholars for Worker Justice, *http://www.catholicscholarsfor workerjustice.org/*.

Academic resources from scholars of Catholic theology and ethics on worker justice.

Economic Justice and the Preferential Option for the Poor

Introduction

The preferential option for the poor, which calls for putting the needs of people who are poor and vulnerable ahead of the needs of others, is a principle that can be traced back to the Hebrew Bible and the foundations of Christianity; however, it was not explicitly named in Catholic social teaching (CST) until recently. While the language of the preferential option for the poor does not appear in early social encyclicals, the principle is present implicitly whenever the teaching pays particular attention to the needs of the most vulnerable members of society. This attention reflects the central meaning of the preferential option for the poor—the people with the most need of solidarity and justice require the greatest response. Often described as the option for the poor and vulnerable, the application of this principle goes beyond the context of economic poverty to recognize other factors that can lead to marginalization, preventing people from full participation in society. Consider your understanding of poverty and the factors that lead people to impoverishment.

- What are some of the causes of poverty? What are some of the ways impoverishment affects people?
- Identify some pathways a person might take to get out poverty. What obstacles might make following these pathways difficult? Who is responsible for alleviating poverty?

- Have you been involved in a service-learning setting that challenged or affirmed any of your ideas or assumptions about poverty?

This chapter will focus specifically on the issue of material poverty and examine the Catholic Church's teachings on economic justice. Consider your understanding of the economy and what economic justice means to you, using the following questions:

- What is the purpose of the economy? What signs indicate that a nation's economy is achieving its purpose?
- Who benefits the most and the least from the US economy as it is currently structured?
- What is economic justice? What values, principles, and priorities shape your understanding of economic justice?

This chapter will trace the development of the principle of the preferential option for the poor in Catholic social tradition first by examining the influence of the bishops' conference of Latin America in conversation with the work of theologians and biblical scholars in articulating the preferential option for the poor. The theological reflection and action for justice that emerged in the context of Central and South America during the decades following Vatican II helped facilitate a shift in CST toward an explicit articulation of the preferential option for the poor.

This chapter will continue by discussing the United States Conference of Catholic Bishops' (USCCB) application of the principle of the preferential option for the poor in addressing poverty in the United States, giving particular attention to their 1986 pastoral letter *Economic Justice for All*. The principles laid out in *Economic Justice for All*, particularly the preferential option for the poor, are made visible in the USCCB official initiative to address poverty in the United States, the Catholic Campaign for Human Development. Next the chapter will draw on social science data and the work of a contemporary theologian to help service learners better analyze and address poverty in the United States. The final section of the chapter provides a summary followed by a vignette drawn from an actual service-learning setting and a series of questions designed to help readers become more familiar with the see-judge-act process.

Preferential Option for the Poor in Catholic Social Teaching

The Call to Protect the Poor

Before the preferential option for the poor was specifically articulated as a major principle of CST, the early social encyclicals recognized the need to protect and care for the most vulnerable members of society. For example, in writings on the state's role in protecting workers, Popes Pius XI and Leo XIII expressed particular concern for the welfare of women and children, who they regarded as weaker members of society.[1] Also, for example, Pius XI expressed this concern in his 1931 encyclical *Quadragesimo anno* (*The Reconstruction of Social Order*): "The function of the rulers of the State, moreover, is to watch over the community and its parts; but in protecting private individuals in their rights, chief consideration ought to be given to the weak and the poor" (no. 25).

Early CST did not aim for radical social transformation. In *Rerum novarum* (*On the Condition of Labor*, 1891), Leo XIII, who believed that natural inequalities exist in society (no. 34), opposed the socialist agenda of leveling class distinctions. This view had implications for the Catholic Church's teaching on social justice. The early social encyclicals emphasized cooperation between social classes rather than the transformation of class structures in achieving justice for the poor. In *Rerum novarum*, Leo XIII argued that the Church could foster mutual love and goodwill among social classes necessary for eliminating the strife between the wealthy and the working class. He argues, "First of all, there is no intermediary more powerful than religion (whereof the Church is the interpreter and guardian) in drawing the rich and the working class together, by reminding each of its duties to the other, and especially of the obligations of justice" (no. 19).

Later CST recognized that cooperation in unjust situations is difficult and emphasized the role of social transformation in

---

1. Some today criticize early Catholic social teaching for being paternalistic, particularly with respect to women. It is important to locate the early social encyclicals in their historical contexts. Pope Leo XIII, like many people in that time period, believed that women were naturally suited for work in the home, and he wanted to protect this role. Feminist thinkers have pointed out the limitations of this view of women.

promoting justice. Pope Paul VI, reflecting a global perspective and an awareness of the effects of colonization on the developing world, pointed out in *Populorum progressio* (*The Development of Peoples*, 1967) how structural inequalities perpetuate social conflict. With particular attention to the context of Latin America, the pope identified the connection between the suffering caused by extreme economic injustices and revolutionary uprisings.[2]

> The injustice of certain situations cries out for God's attention. Lacking the bare necessities of life, whole nations are under the thumb of others; they cannot act on their own initiative; they cannot exercise personal responsibility; they cannot work toward a higher degree of cultural refinement or a greater participation in social and public life. They are sorely tempted to redress these insults to their human nature by violent means. (no. 30)

Although the pope recognizes in *Populorum progressio* (*PP*) the temptation to resort to violent uprisings, he cautions against it, recognizing that such actions "engender new injustices, introduce new inequities and bring new disasters" (no. 31). Nevertheless, the pope argues for "profound changes" (no. 32) to correct the disparity of wealth perpetuating social conflict in developing countries.

In 1971 Paul VI called a synod (an international gathering of bishops) to address justice in the world. This synod, made up largely of bishops from Latin America, articulated in *Justice in the World* (*JW*) an explicit relationship between the Church's social mission and the transformation of unjust structures. The bishops affirmed that "Action on behalf of justice and participation in the transformation of the world fully appear to us as a constitutive dimension of the

---

2. El Salvador provides an example of the context to which Pope Paul VI was likely addressing in *Populorum progressio*. During the 1970s and 1980s a military-led government backed by the interests of a few wealthy landowners, assisted by US military aid, violently resisted movements for reform of the country's oppressive economic inequalities. The conflict between the military government and the revolutionary guerrilla groups fueled a long civil war (1979–1992) in which thousands of people were killed or disappeared. For more information on this context, see Anna Lisa Peterson, *Martyrdom and the Politics of Religion: Progressive Catholicism in El Salvador's Civil War* (New York: State University of New York Press, 1997).

preaching of the Gospel" (no. 6). By emphasizing the social implications of the gospel message, the bishops direct the Church toward advocacy for the poor and oppressed. They ground their understanding of justice in a biblical view of God as a liberator of the oppressed: "In the Old Testament God reveals himself to us as the liberator of the oppressed and the defender of the poor, demanding from people faith in him and justice towards one's neighbor" (no. 30).

Pope Francis has made the preferential option for the poor and vulnerable a top priority of his papacy, declaring in his inaugural public address that he wants "a poor church for the poor." He elaborated on this desire in his 2013 apostolic exhortation *Evangelii gaudium* (*On the Proclamation of the Gospel in Today's World*). Francis wants the Church to be transformed by the poor because, as they experience God responding to their suffering with solidarity, they have a unique understanding of the Gospel. The pope invites the Church to "find Christ in them, to lend our voice to their causes, but also to be their friends, to listen to them, to speak for them and to embrace the mysterious wisdom which God wishes to share with us through them" (*EG*, 198).

For Francis, solidarity with the poor should not only transform the Church but also should transform unjust structures that perpetuate poverty. As the first pope from Latin America, Pope Francis has witnessed the devastating effects of poverty, and this awareness grounds his strong critique of economic inequality. "Just as the commandment 'Thou shalt not kill' sets a clear limit in order to safeguard the value of human life, today we also have to say 'thou shalt not' to an economy of exclusion and inequality. Such an economy kills" (*EG*, 53). Recognizing poverty as a form of social exclusion, the preferential option for the poor also means "Each individual Christian and every community is called to be an instrument of God for the liberation and promotion of the poor, and for enabling them to be fully a part of society" (*EG*, 187).

This section traced an important shift in CST that lays a foundation for the Catholic Church's contemporary understanding of the preferential option for the poor. The early social encyclicals of Leo XIII and Pius XI positioned the Church as a mediator between the rich and the poor, emphasizing the need for harmony and mutual respect between social classes. Following the writings of Paul VI,

Pope Francis invited a group of people living unhoused near the Vatican to a private tour of the Sistine Chapel in March 2015. In his actions and words, Francis has challenged the Catholic Church to exercise a preferential option for the poor.

the 1971 synod of bishops observed that poverty oppressed people by limiting their ability to develop and flourish. Subsequent to this observation, the Catholic Church has positioned itself as an advocate for the poor and vulnerable. Pope Francis exemplifies this position in his teaching and action.

The Contribution of Liberation Theology

A theological shift in the middle of the twentieth century shaped the Catholic Church's contemporary understanding of the preferential option for the poor. The shift involved the growing realization that theology is contextual, reflecting the historical and cultural realities out of which it emerges. The Second Vatican Council (1962–1965), which drew attention to both the importance of history as theological context and the Catholic Church's global nature, opened the doors for the emergence of new theologies that consider people's situation in life. This shift provided the context for the development of liberation theology, which aims to see reality from the perspective of the poor and the vulnerable and lifts up the preferential option for the poor as a key component of what it means to be Christian.

When liberation theologians refer to poverty, they are not viewing poverty as a state of holiness that many have tried to achieve by embracing a life of simplicity. Rather, liberation theologians refer to poverty as an immediate reality that causes great suffering and may even impel faithful Christians to wonder if God is punishing them. When liberation theology emerged out of Latin America during the 1970s and 1980s, poverty was a leading cause of death in many Latin American communities. Out of this context, liberation theologians named poverty as a reality that diminishes human dignity and opposes life. One of the early voices in liberation theology was that of Peruvian priest Gustavo Gutierrez. He speaks to this perspective:

> Life, a gift from God, is also the first human right. The poverty and insignificance in which many people live violates that right. In effect, poverty means death, both physical death that is early and unjust, due to lack of the most basic necessities for life, and cultural death, as expressed in oppression and discrimination for reasons of race, culture or gender.[3]

Liberation theologians view poverty as a negation of life and therefore speak of it as a sin, specifically as a social sin because it is perpetuated by social structures and institutions (i.e., economic markets, trade agreements, tax policies, etc.). Redemption from social sin requires a transformation of the unjust structures that perpetuate the harm. This realization provides the basis for framing the Christian theme of salvation as liberation. Liberation theologians invite Christians to consider how God's redemptive action occurs not only in a personal relationship with Christ or in God's final judgment at the end of time but also in the midst of human history through the building of the kingdom of God. This realization provides a focus for the mission of the Catholic Church.

---

3. Gustavo Gutierrez, "Memory and Prophecy," in *Option for the Poor in Christian Theology*, ed. Daniel Groody (Notre Dame, IN: University of Notre Dame Press, 2007), 27.

El Salvador Martyrs

Liberation theology emerged not only through ideas but also through concrete actions for justice. Sometimes such actions threaten people who benefit from unjust structures. In the context of the Salvadoran civil war (1979–1992) and the conflict that preceded it, Church leaders became targets of military violence because of their advocacy for the poor. Many people consider these individuals to be martyrs (people who die as a result of their commitment to their faith). Archbishop Oscar Romero, who spoke against the repressive military government, was assassinated by a Salvadoran soldier in 1980. In 1989, six Jesuit priests, along with their housekeeper and her daughter, were assassinated in their home by a US-trained Salvadoran soldier. The murders prompted many US citizens to examine their country's involvement in supporting and training the Salvadoran military. The Ignatian Solidarity Network developed in response to this issue and continues to commemorate the deaths of the Salvadoran martyrs as they advocate for social justice.[4]

A meeting of the bishops' conference of Latin America (Consejo Episcopal Latinoamericano or CELAM) in 1968 at Medellín, Colombia, was important in the history of the Catholic Church and for CST. At Medellín, the bishops identified justice for the poor as a biblical mandate and made working for justice on behalf of the poor a priority. Echoing liberation theologians, the bishops associated poverty with structural injustices that perpetuate a cycle of marginalization and state-sponsored violence against people who called for reform. They use the language of liberation to describe God's action in history.

> The Latin American Church has a message for all men on this continent who 'hunger and thirst after justice.' The very God who creates men in his image and likeness, creates the 'earth and all that is in it for the use of all men and all nations, in such a way that created goods can reach all in a

---

4. See the Ignatian Solidarity Network's website.

more just manner,' and gives them power to transform and perfect the world in solidarity. It is the same God who, in the fullness of time, sends his Son in the flesh, so that He might come to liberate all men from the slavery to which sin has subjected them: hunger, misery, oppression and ignorance, in a word, that injustice and hatred which have their origin in human selfishness.[5]

The observation that social and economic structures oppress people living in poverty provides the rationale for the preferential option for the poor. Some people find the language of the preferential option for the poor to be confusing or misleading. To say that God prefers some people over others seems to imply that God's love is subject to the same limitations as human love, suggesting that God's love is partial and prejudiced. Liberation theologians do not use this language to undermine the belief that God's love is universal, maximal, and nondiscriminatory. Rather, they argue that God offers a preferential concern for the poor because social structures disadvantage them. Biblical scholar Elsa Tamez explains this as follows:

> We say that the option of God for the poor is preferential in the sense that God loves all of God's creatures but has a preferential or special love for the poor precisely because of their disadvantaged position in an unequal and discriminating society. . . . The foundation of the option for the poor is the intention to end structural sin that produces dehumanization of the poor as well as those responsible for their poverty. In other words, we can affirm that precisely because the love of God is universal, God opts for the poor so that there may no longer be excluded persons in society.[6]

Liberation theology draws on the biblical understanding of the preferential option for the poor and places it at the center of the Church's social mission.

---

5. CELAM, "Documents from Medellin," in *Renewing the Earth: Catholic Documents on Peace, Justice and Liberation*, eds. David O'Brien and Thomas Shannon (New York: Doubleday, 1977), 3.

6. Elsa Tamez, "Poverty, the Poor and the Option for the Poor," in *Option for the Poor*, ed. Groody, 46.

The Reception of Liberation Theology

Liberation theology developed through the work of professional theologians such as Gustavo Gutierrez, the Latin American bishops, and laywomen and laymen who reflected on the meaning of the experiences of those who were poor in light of the gospel. The theology that emerged has not always been fully received by official leaders of the Catholic Church. In 1984, during the papacy of John Paul II, when Joseph Ratzinger (who became Pope Benedict XVI) was prefect for the Congregation for the Doctrine of the Faith, the Vatican issued a statement, "Instruction on Certain Aspects of the 'Theology of Liberation.'" The document criticized some theologies of liberation for incorporating Marxist themes "not compatible with the Christian conception of humanity and society" (section VII, no. 8).[7] The instruction does, however, embrace the principle of the option for the poor, which became a more pronounced theme of CST after the development of liberation theology. This principle is now widely regarded as integral to the Christian message. Benedict XVI reflected this in a 2007 statement: "the preferential option for the poor is implicit in the Christological faith in the God who became poor for us, so as to enrich us with his poverty (cf. 2 Cor 8:9)."[8]

The United States Conference of Catholic Bishops on the Economy

The USCCB applied CST, including the principle of the preferential option for the poor, to economic life in their 1986 pastoral letter, *Economic Justice for All*. This section will examine the major themes of that text and highlight how these themes inform the bishops' anti-poverty initiative, the Catholic Campaign for Human Development.

---

7. Congregation for the Doctrine of the Faith, "Instruction on Certain Aspects of the 'Theology of Liberation'" (Libreria Editrice Vaticana, 1984).

8. Pope Benedict XVI, Address of His Holiness Benedict XVI to the Bishops of Latin America and the Caribbean, Shrine of Aparecida, May 13, 2007, no. 3, available at *http://www.vatican.va/holy_father/benedict_xvi/speeches/2007/may/documents/hf_ben-xvi_spe_20070513_conference-aparecida_en.html*.

The Context of *Economic Justice for All*

When the bishops formed a committee to draft a pastoral letter on economic justice in 1980, they intended to focus on a critique of Marxism. Archbishop Rembert Weakland, the chair of the committee, pushed the members to focus on the moral dimensions of capitalism instead, noting that this would be more relevant and challenging to the US context.[9] The committee's work coincided with the presidency of Ronald Reagan (1981–1989), whose approach to economics relied on tax cuts intended to increase consumer spending. Reagan, and others, advocated for little government interference in order to promote freedom in the market. Many Americans believe that this *laissez-faire* ("let it be") approach to capitalism results in a strong economy that ultimately benefits the whole society, while others critique unregulated free-market capitalism for prioritizing profit over the common good and leaving the impoverished behind without a safety net.

Since *Rerum novarum* (*On the Condition of Labor*), CST has offered a sustained critique of both liberal capitalism and socialism. The USCCB follows this tradition by neither endorsing nor fundamentally rejecting particular economic systems, nor do they attempt to create a new economy based on the principles of Catholic teaching. Rather, they draw on the themes of Catholic social thought, particularly human dignity, the call to community and participation, solidarity, and the preferential option for the poor, to develop a framework for economic justice.

Though the USCCB did not endorse or reject particular economic systems in the document, they did offer critiques and concrete suggestions for how to improve the capitalist system of the United States. In doing so, the bishops recognized that they were taking a stance on a controversial matter, and they anticipated that there would be debates among Catholics on the moral authority of their recommendations. The bishops identify their statements as *prudential judgments*, a term used in Catholic moral theology to distinguish reasonable suggestions on moral life from authoritative declarations

---

9. Charles Curran, "Reception of Economic Teaching in the United States," in *Modern Catholic Social Teaching: Commentaries and Interpretations*, ed. Kenneth Himes et al. (Washington, DC: Georgetown University Press, 2005), 478.

about what is morally good or evil. In *Economic Justice for All* (*EJA*) they state,

> We know that some of our specific recommendations are controversial. As bishops, we do not claim to make these prudential judgments with the same kind of authority that marks our declarations of principle. But we feel obliged to teach by example how Christians can undertake concrete analysis and make specific judgments on economic issues. The church's teachings cannot be left at the level of appealing generalities. (no. 20)

The bishops are careful to distinguish prudential judgments from authoritative moral principles for a couple of reasons. First, they recognize that Catholics of good conscience can disagree on how to apply the principles of CST in actual contexts. The bishops claim to avoid dictating how Catholics should vote, recognizing the legitimate separation of church and state. Second, they identify themselves as religious leaders, as experts on Catholic faith and morality, not as economists, sociologists, or political scientists. Speaking to this, the USCCB states the following:

> In our letter, we write as pastors, not public officials. We speak as moral teachers, not economic technicians. We seek not to make some political or ideological point but to lift up the human and ethical dimensions of economic life, aspects too often neglected in public discussion. We bring to this task a dual heritage of Catholic social teaching and traditional American values. (*EJA*, no. 7)

Like the US bishops' 1983 pastoral letter on peace, *Economic Justice for All* was the result of a broad consultative effort that sought to integrate multiple perspectives. The bishops relied on the expertise of many others, including economists, workers, business owners, ministers, activists, and theologians. They describe the process of drafting the letter as involving "careful inquiry, wide consultation, and prayerful discernment" (*EJA*, no. 3), noting that they were enriched by the listening process. The result of this effort was nearly one hundred pages of analysis of the economic context of the United States, with theological, biblical, and ethical reflection on that context. The bishops also made constructive suggestions for developing a more just US economy, describing their proposal as "a New American Experiment." The bishops' new American experiment was framed as a full realization of democracy, one that allowed everyone to participate in the American dream (*EJA*, nos. 295–297).

Themes of *Economic Justice for All*

The theme of participation is central to the bishops' vision of economic justice, and it provides a focus for organizing the major principles of the letter, including the principle of the preferential option for the poor. The bishops state boldly, "We judge any economic system by what it does *for* and *to* people and by how it permits all to *participate* in it" (*EJA*, no. 13). There are many ways a society can evaluate its economy. It can evaluate an economy based on how it promotes profit, production, or distribution. By naming participation as the criterion for judging an economy, however, the bishops are offering a personalist perspective on economic life, summed up in the statement, "The economy should serve people, not the other way around" (*EJA*, no. 13). Implicit in their statement are the following assumptions, which they directly state: that the economy has moral dimensions because it is a human activity and that the human dimension cannot simply be considered alongside other dimensions of the economy. A personalist approach to the economy argues that the human dimension must be the center of all economic life.

The bishops' focus on participation has a firm grounding in the Catholic social tradition, particularly in light of the principle of the call to community. The bishops emphasize participation within the community because of the theological assumption that God created human beings for relationship, making persons inherently social. Following the assumption that people are social beings, to exclude an individual from the life of community can be considered a violation of human potential. There are many ways an individual can be prevented from participating in the economic life of a community. The bishops describe patterns of economic exclusion.

> Within the United States, individuals, families, and local communities fall victim to a downward cycle of poverty generated by economic forces they are powerless to influence. The poor, the disabled, and the unemployed too often

are simply left behind. . . . These patterns of exclusion are created by free human beings. In this sense they can be called forms of social sin. (*EJA*, no. 77)

By describing marginalization from the community as a form of social sin, the bishops link the Church's social mission with the work to overcome economic injustices. Again, social sin refers to the structures of injustice that perpetuate racism, sexism, and poverty. Redemption from social sin requires a transformation of unjust structures. In this case, the bishops are inviting people to participate in overcoming the social sins engendered in the cycle of poverty.

The right to participate in community is grounded in the principle of the common good as developed in CST. The bishops' insistence that everyone has the right and responsibility to participate in the common good provides a basic argument for the preferential option for the poor. When individuals are empowered to participate in social life, they strengthen the whole community. Recall that the Catholic social tradition refers to the common good to point to all that is produced in social life that allows the whole community to flourish. Although people rightly pursue a good life as individuals, CST calls people to pursue the common good. According to CST, the common good is not measured by the greatest good for the majority but rather by the flourishing of everyone. The commitment to the common good, therefore, involves a preferential commitment to the flourishing of the poor and vulnerable of a community.

The bishops offer a biblical and theological mandate for the preferential option for the poor in *Economic Justice for All*.

Though in the Gospels and in the New Testament as a whole the offer of salvation is extended to all peoples, Jesus takes the side of those most in need, physically and spiritually. The example of Jesus poses a number of challenges to the contemporary Church. It imposes a prophetic mandate to speak for those who have no one to speak for them, to be a defender of the defenseless, who in biblical terms are the poor. It also demands a compassionate vision that enables the Church to see things from the side of the poor and powerless and to assess lifestyle, policies, and social institutions in terms of their impact on the poor. It summons the Church also to be

> an instrument in assisting people to experience the liberating
> power of God in their own lives so that they may respond to
> the Gospel in freedom and in dignity. (no. 52)

Drawing on Scripture, the bishops provide four points that summarize the grounds for and meaning of the preferential option for the
poor in Catholic social thought. First, Jesus provides the mandate for
the preferential option for the poor through his own example. Second, the biblical notion of poverty is connected to the state of power-
lessness and marginalization. Third, the poor and vulnerable provide
a vantage point from which to evaluate social structures and policies.
Fourth, the Church's social mission involves being an instrument of
God's liberating love for the vulnerable.

Catholic Campaign for Human Development

The USCCB's commitment to alleviating poverty predates their articulation of economic justice in 1986 in *Economic Justice for All*. One of
the most successful of the bishops' efforts is the Catholic Campaign
for Human Development (CCHD), the largest privately funded self-
help program for people living in poverty in the United States. The
CCHD has distributed more than $400 million to various groups
since its establishment in 1970. Unlike other Catholic-sponsored
charitable organizations that offer direct assistance to those living in
poverty, the CCHD's emphasis on social justice looks for long-term
solutions that address the roots of poverty. The CCHD has developed
into a unique program that directs its efforts to the empowerment of
impoverished communities through self-led projects aimed at social
change. Specifically, it funds community organizing efforts, new businesses in impoverished communities, and nonprofit programs that are
led by the people most affected by the service. The USCCB manifests
the principle of participation in the way they direct CCHD funds:

> For the purposes of CCHD funding, the participation of
> poor people in the shaping and ongoing direction of orga-
> nizations is a central criterion. While "advisory" groups may
> also strengthen an organization, poor and low income peo-
> ple must have and maintain a strong voice in the organiza-
> tion's leadership both in terms of its governance structure

and policy decisions, specially through their direct participation in the board of directors.[10]

Although the CCHD funds programs run by organizations that are not Catholic, it requires recipients to agree to promote the principles of Catholic social thought. In addition, the bishops see the CCHD as a vehicle to promote subsidiarity: "[The] CCHD focuses on local communities seeking to give voice to those closest to problems of poverty, as these communities address economic injustice working with local, state or national institutions to address the causes of poverty."[11] The rationale behind subsidiarity is that the people who are the most affected by social issues are the ones who have the best understanding of what they need. Following this rationale, social change should be led by the individuals most immediately affected by that change. Guided by the principle of subsidiarity and the preferential option for the poor, this approach to poverty promotes participation among communities that have been marginalized.

The Catholic Worker Movement

The Catholic Worker movement is one of the most well-known lay-led Catholic initiatives to serve and advocate for people living in poverty. Activist and journalist Dorothy Day started the Catholic Worker with her friend, Peter Maurin, in 1933 as a way to provide hospitality and basic necessities to people living in poverty. Day and other Catholic Workers embraced radical simplicity to live in community with the poor. *The Catholic Worker* was also the name of the newspaper they founded to promote nonviolence and social justice from a Catholic perspective. Today, the Catholic Worker movement includes many small communities across the United States that, inspired by the gospel and the example of Dorothy Day, choose to live and serve alongside people living in poverty.

---

10. CCHD Basic Principles of Catholic Mission, available at *http://www.usccb.org /about/catholic-campaign-for-human-development/grants/cchd-basic-principles-of-catholic -mission.cfm.*

11. CCHD, "Catholic Identity," available at *http://www.usccb.org/about/catholic -campaign-for-human-development/frequently-asked-questions.cfm.*

Reading the Signs of the Times: Poverty and Empowerment

This section will further explore poverty and economic life in the United States, focusing particularly on wealth inequality. It will provide information about the widening gap between the wealthy and the impoverished that can contribute to contemporary social analysis, and it will explore theologian James Bailey's use of Catholic social thought to advocate for empowering the poor through asset building.

In the winter of 2013, protesters around the Bay Area organized a series of actions aimed to block commuter buses headed to the Silicon Valley-based offices of Google, Facebook, and Apple. The protests, which gained national attention, were not only about getting tech companies to pay the city to park the large commuter coaches on crowded city streets. Rather, the protesters aimed to draw attention to the income inequality, cost of living, and shortage of affordable housing in the Bay Area.[12] One can debate the role of tech companies such as Google and Twitter in addressing these problems, but one cannot ignore the hard realities cities like San Francisco face with the widening gap between those with high incomes and those with the lowest incomes. A recent analysis by Bloomberg demonstrated a rapid widening of income inequality between 2010 and 2015. The analysis compares the 20 percent highest and 20 percent lowest earners across a number of cities. San Francisco, Seattle, San Jose, and other metropolitan hubs for the tech industry saw the most dramatic disparity between the rich and the poor.[13]

The shrinking middle class and growing wealth gap in the United States poses a number of ethical concerns. First, many people are unable to own their own homes and make long-term investments. Without the opportunity to build assets (homeownership, retirement, etc.), low-income people have limited opportunities

---

12. Casey Minor, "In a Divided San Francisco, Private Tech Buses Drive Tension," *All Things Considered*, National Public Radio (December 17, 2013). Available at *http://www.npr.org/sections/alltechconsidered/2013/12/17/251960183/in-a-divided-san-francisco-private-tech-buses-drive-tension*.

13. Vincent Del Giudice and Wei Lu, "America's Rich Get Richer and the Poor Get Replaced by Robots," in *Bloomberg* (April 26, 2017), available at *https://www.bloomberg.com/news/articles/2017-04-26/america-s-rich-poor-divide-keeps-ballooning-as-robots-take-jobs*.

to rise out of poverty. The US government provides a number of asset-building incentives—tax deductions or exemptions for mortgage interest, financial investments, and 401k retirement savings. However, many of these incentives exclude people who are unemployed, underemployed, or whose income does not allow them to make long-term investments. Theologian James Bailey points out the injustice of this situation, arguing the following:

> The United States already has in place a variety of initiatives that, taken together, constitute a vigorous and broad-based asset-building policy. The problem is that the beneficiaries of these policies are almost exclusively the nonpoor. Indeed, the current asset-based initiatives are so focused on the nonpoor that it would be accurate to characterize them as a "preferential option for the nonpoor."[14]

Bailey does not argue for an end to such asset-building programs, but rather stresses the need for broader participation among lower-income people. He sees asset building as an essential way to empower people to escape the cycle of poverty.

Bailey draws on Catholic social thought to emphasize the importance of asset building to alleviate poverty. Specifically, he argues that the themes of the common good, participation, and the preferential option for the poor all encourage broadened ownership and wealth distribution. Catholic social thought, he argues, also provides a framework for economic life that challenges the individualism that fuels the wealth gap in the United States. Referring to the common good, Bailey writes, "To the degree that ownership is correlated with greater participation at all levels of society, expanding the number of owners not only contributes to the individual good of these new owners but also to the good of all members of society."[15] This understanding of ownership fits well with the USCCB's emphasis on participation as a central characteristic of a just economy. It also speaks to the importance of the preferential option for the poor because within the framework of the common good, empowering the economically marginalized contributes to the flourishing of all.

---

14. James Bailey, *Rethinking Poverty: Income, Assets, and the Catholic Social Justice Tradition* (Notre Dame, IN: University of Notre Dame Press, 2010), 18.

15. Ibid., 49.

Summary and Integration for Service Learners

This chapter traced the development of the preferential option for the poor in the Catholic social tradition. Rooted in Scripture, this theme became prominent in Catholic social thought through the influence of Latin American liberation theology. Today, the preferential option for the poor provides a basis for contemporary CST on economic justice. This is especially evident in the way that the USCCB has addressed poverty and economic life in the United States. This chapter also explored the USCCB's response to poverty through CCHD and the bishops' concern about the inequalities between the wealthy and impoverished in the United States today. Now that you have learned about CST as it relates to poverty and economic justice, revisit your responses to the questions at the beginning of this chapter. Would you answer any questions differently? Has the chapter challenged any of your ideas or assumptions about poverty and what should be done to address it? Use the following story of social change and questions to practice aspects of the see-judge-act process in relation to this topic.

See, Judge, Act in the Community

Vignette

As director of engagement for a community-based nonprofit organization that empowers youth and their families through education, Dani is passionate about helping service learners and interns learn about the Western Addition neighborhood of San Francisco—the history, culture, and social issues that impact the historically African American district. After a guided orientation to the neighborhood, a group of students from a Jesuit Catholic high school shared their observations and questions. During the orientation, they encountered eight public and subsidized housing developments. A number of students noted that they had never seen a public housing development even though they were born and raised in San Francisco. Two students shared that they grew up familiar with public housing, but weren't surprised that their classmates had never encountered it. The group also noted changes to the neighborhood, such as new luxury condo buildings and trendy shops. Working with a diverse group of high school and university students, Dani sees her job as helping them ask the kinds of questions that not only gather information but also promote self-awareness and growth in understanding the perspective of others, as well as the established systems that often keep some groups at the margins.

See: Social Analysis

- How might economic background have influenced the different reactions to the neighborhood among students?
- What are some of the questions one should ask to better understand how and why public housing is structured in a particular way?

Judge: Ethical Reflection

- Drawing upon the principles of the common good and participation, what concerns would you raise in evaluating the impact of gentrification on this neighborhood?
- What would solidarity look like in this situation? What attitudes and actions could the various stakeholders take to express solidarity?

Act: Promoting Justice

- Based on what you have learned about CST's option for the poor and poverty in the United States today, what ideas might you have for alleviating poverty? What elements are essential for an antipoverty measure to work?
- How do you distinguish actions oriented toward charity and those oriented toward social justice? From your perspective, what is the role of each in implementing the principle of CST that calls for giving preference to the poor?

Suggestions for Further Social Analysis in a Service-Learning Context

- Using recent census data, research the median income for the neighborhood in which a service-learning setting you are familiar with is located. How does this income data compare with data for the United States in general and for the state and city in which the neighborhood is located?

- Identify some programs (private and public) aimed at assisting the poor or alleviating poverty or spurring economic growth in a particular locale. Establish criteria for assessing the success of these programs, and then evaluate them on that basis. What factors contribute to success?

- Compare the median income of people living in the neighborhood in which a service-learning setting you are familiar with is located with the estimated living expenses offered by the Consumer Expenditure Survey (*https://www.bls.gov/cex/*) for the same geographic area. What do you notice?

For Further Study on Catholic Social Thought and Poverty

Printed Materials

Bailey, James. *Rethinking Poverty: Income, Assets, and the Catholic Social Justice Tradition.* Notre Dame, IN: University of Notre Dame Press, 2010.

Bane, Mary Jo, and Lawrence Mead. *Lifting Up the Poor: A Dialogue on Religion, Poverty and Welfare Reform.* Washington, DC: Brookings Institution Press, 2003.

Groody, Daniel G., ed. *The Option for the Poor in Christian Theology.* Notre Dame, IN: University of Notre Dame Press, 2007.

Massaro, Thomas. *United States Welfare Policy: A Catholic Response.* Washington, DC: Georgetown University Press, 2007.

O' Neill, William. "Poverty in the United States." In *Resources for Social and Cultural Analysis: Reading the Signs of the Times,* eds. T. Howland Sanks and John Coleman. New York: Paulist Press, 1993.

Websites

Catholic Campaign for Human Development, *http://www.usccb.org /about/catholic-campaign-for-human-development/.*

The US bishops' antipoverty initiative highlights stories of social change and offers resources to learn about poverty in the United States.

Catholics Confront Global Poverty, *http://www.confrontglobal poverty.org/.*

Sponsored by the US bishops and Catholic Relief Services, this website provides resources for education and action related to poverty, climate change, and migration.

Catholic Worker, *http://www.catholicworker.org/.*

Offers information on Dorothy Day, Peter Maurin, and the international network of Catholic Worker communities.

Promoting Solidarity in Peacemaking

Introduction

The concept of *solidarity* is used generally to describe people's interdependence and their responsibility to act in ways that enhance their relationships with others. Solidarity challenges everyone to recognize all the ways that people are linked together and to strengthen the bonds that promote the good of all. Various leaders have at times used the value of solidarity as a rallying cry to encourage people to participate in works for the good of others, such as social movements, labor unions, the promotion of economic justice, and efforts to provide assistance across the globe. Reflect on your understanding of interdependence and solidarity and consider how you might connect these understandings to a service-learning setting.

- How do you define interdependence? Can you identify an example that illustrates the depth of the interdependence of people in your community? In what ways does the concept of *solidarity* cohere with or differ from your understanding of interdependence?

- Has your understanding of interdependence developed or changed in light of a service-learning experience you may have had? Have you encountered people acting in solidarity with others in a service-learning setting? Explain.

- Have you met people in a service-learning setting who have suffered injustice because they or others have ignored their interdependence with others? If so, what social issues seem to emerge from this? What information would you need to better identify, understand, and respond to these issues?

Catholic social teaching (CST) uses the principle of solidarity to articulate people's responsibility to respond to many injustices, including economic inequalities, abuse of the environment, unjust wars and violence, and human-rights violations. This chapter will focus on how the principle of solidarity has informed the United States Conference of Catholic Bishops' (USCCB) response to violence through the promotion of peace. As a global and local problem, violence breaks down communities, damages solidarity, and diminishes recognition of human dignity. Violence and its consequences affect communities in many ways. Consider how these may be affecting your community and people you may be familiar with through service learning.

- Has the community in which you live been affected by violence, such as abuse, exploitation, violent crime, or war? If so, has the community addressed this violence? Explain how.

- Have you met people in a service-learning setting who have been affected by violence? If so, has the community within which these people live addressed the violence? What information would you need to assess the effects violence may have on the people in this service-learning setting?

- What are some of the ways peace is maintained among the people you interact with most closely? How do these ways of maintaining peace compare with those used by people in a service-learning setting with which you are familiar? Who takes responsibility for maintaining peace? What resources or skills do they use? What strategies promote peace effectively?

This chapter will examine how CST articulates the meaning and significance of solidarity and explore how this principle is applied by the USCCB in their response to violence. In their 1983 pastoral letter, *The Challenge of Peace: God's Promise and Our Response*, the USCCB addresses the moral dimensions of war, and drawing on the Catholic social tradition, they challenge people to promote peace. Ten years after *Challenge of Peace*, the USCCB issued another statement, *The Harvest of Justice Is Sown in Peace*, which echoes many themes of the earlier pastoral letter but also reveals some significant developments.

War, violence, and their consequences continue to pose new and evolving ethical problems in the United States.

Next the chapter will examine some of the issues that US veterans face today, drawing on social science data and insights from Christian ethics. The final section of the chapter provides a summary followed by a vignette drawn from an actual service-learning setting and a series of questions designed to help readers practice aspects of the see-judge-act process.

The Principle of Solidarity in Catholic Social Teaching

Foundations of Solidarity in Early Teachings

The early social encyclicals do not rely on the word *solidarity*; however, the theme of human interdependence runs throughout the texts. Popes Leo XIII and Pius XI regard human interdependence as a reality and argue that society must reflect this unity through the peaceful cooperation of people from all social classes. The popes envisioned this cooperation being promoted with a spirit of benevolence through charitable practices. Pius XI argued that charity could not replace justice, understood as giving each person his or her due. However, charity, the pope argued, is indispensable because it promotes a sense of unity and commitment to the common good, which justice alone cannot achieve. Justice is important because it challenges people to recognize their obligation to the common good, and charity is essential because it promotes feelings of love and benevolence, which foster a sense of unity and kinship within society. Pius XI suggests in *Quadragesimo anno* (*The Reconstruction of Social Order*, 1931), "And so, then only will true cooperation be possible for a single common good when the constituent parts of society deeply feel themselves members of one great family and children of the same Heavenly Father" (no. 137).

International Solidarity as the Foundation for Peace

The early social encyclicals tended to focus on issues affecting the European Catholic Church. As CST became more international in scope, the concept of *solidarity* become more prominent in this teaching. Pope John XXIII was important in facilitating this shift. In 1961 he used the language of solidarity to address the responsibilities of wealthy, powerful nations toward impoverished ones. In *Mater et magistra* (*Christianity and Social Progress*, 1961), he states: "The solidarity which binds all . . . together as members of a common family makes it impossible for wealthy nations to look with indifference on the hunger, misery and poverty of other nations whose citizens are unable to enjoy even elementary human rights" (no. 157). John XXIII reflected on the connection between the promotion of human rights and peacebuilding in his encyclical *Pacem in terris* (*Peace on Earth*, 1963). According to the pope, human rights include cultural, political, and economic rights. He argues that nations should promote human rights in the spirit of solidarity, collaborating as much as possible for the common good of the entire human family (see *Pacem in terris*, no. 98). Reflecting his global perspective, John XXIII's encyclicals stress the importance of international solidarity in the pursuit of human development.

In *Populorum progressio* (*The Development of Peoples*, 1967), Pope Paul VI explicitly develops the connection between the promotion of human rights throughout the world and peacebuilding, exemplified in his often-quoted statement, "If you want peace, work for justice."[1] Recall that justice, from the perspective of Paul VI, could be achieved only through integral human development, development that extends beyond economic growth to the many dimensions of the human person. Promoting full human development, the pope insists in *Populorum progressio* (*PP*), is a responsibility of all nations and ultimately benefits every nation because it is the key to securing lasting peace:

> When we fight poverty and oppose the unfair conditions of the present, we are not just promoting human well-being; we are also furthering . . . spiritual and moral development, and hence we are benefiting the whole human race. For peace is not simply the absence of warfare, based on a precarious balance of power; it is fashioned by efforts

---

1. Pope Paul VI, "World Day for Peace Message" (1972), available at *http://w2.vatican.va/content/paul-vi/en/messages/peace/documents/hf_p-vi_mes_19711208_v-world-day-for-peace.html*.

directed day after day toward the establishment of the ordered universe willed by God, with a more perfect form of justice. (no. 76)

Paul VI connects the pursuit of peace with the alleviation of poverty and injustice—peace is not just the absence of war. Lasting peace can be achieved only by securing human rights and promoting integral human development. In CST, the principle of solidarity provides a rationale for international cooperation in this effort: by broadening one's responsibility for others beyond national, cultural, and ethnic boundaries, the work of promoting global justice becomes a responsibility of all.

Solidarity as a Christian Virtue

Pope John Paul II wrote on the topic of solidarity in *Sollicitudo rei socialis* (*On Social Concern*, 1987), his encyclical commemorating the twentieth anniversary of Paul VI's *Populorum progressio* (*The Development of Peoples*). In *Sollicitudo rei socialis* (*SRS*), John Paul II echoed many of his predecessor's insights on the connection between peace and international justice. John Paul II also retrieved insights from the early social encyclicals, emphasizing the role of charity in promoting a sense of unity necessary for the promotion of solidarity. The pope suggests that solidarity embraces the demands of justice but also goes beyond these demands by incorporating a spirit of generosity, which is rooted in his understanding of Christian discipleship.

> In what has been said so far it has been possible to identify many points of contact between solidarity and charity, which is the distinguishing mark of Christ's disciples (cf. John 13:35). In the light of faith, solidarity seeks to go beyond itself, to take on the specifically Christian dimension of total gratuity, forgiveness and reconciliation. (*SRS*, no. 40)

John Paul II connects solidarity to Christian discipleship in two ways—providing a theological understanding of solidarity and describing solidarity as a virtue, an expression of moral life. He roots solidarity in the theological understanding that all people are part of a single family that exists in relationship with the one God, creator of all. The second Creation narrative in Genesis conveys this understanding by asserting that it is not good for a person to be alone (see Genesis 2:18). Christians interpret this to mean that human beings need relationships to thrive and develop. In light of this theological understanding, human interdependence is not accidental or a weakness to overcome. Rather, interdependence is rooted in God's intention that relationships have a central role in human existence.

John Paul II develops this theological understanding further by pointing out that because people are created in the image and likeness of God the Trinity, they are called to reflect the loving communion that characterizes the relationships among the three persons of the Trinity.

> Beyond human and natural bonds, already so close and strong, there is discerned in the light of faith a new model of the unity of the human race, which must ultimately inspire our solidarity. This supreme model of unity, which is a reflection of the intimate life of God, one God in three Persons, is what we Christians mean by the word "communion." (*SRS*, no. 40)

This theological understanding of human relationships carries moral implications. Communion, as modeled in the life of the Trinity, provides a model for human relationships. These relationships are marked by love, mutuality, and commitment to the flourishing of the other. According to this model, people, being in God's image, should reflect these qualities in all aspects of their lives, which are inherently social.

The second way John Paul II connects solidarity to Christian discipleship is by presenting solidarity as a virtue. Virtues are habits and dispositions that orient people toward a moral good. Honesty, for example, is a virtue that orients a person toward a moral good, telling the truth. Solidarity is also a virtue because it involves habits and dispositions that orient people toward taking responsibility for the common good. Taking responsibility for the common good involves recognizing not only that people are interdependent but also that the reality of interdependence has moral implications. John Paul II suggests,

When interdependence becomes recognized in this way [as a moral reality], the correlative response as a moral and social attitude, as a "virtue," is solidarity. This then is not a feeling of vague compassion or shallow distress at the misfortunes of so many people, both near and far. On the contrary, it is a firm and persevering determination to commit oneself to the common good; that is to say to the good of all and of each individual, because we are all really responsible for all. (*SRS*, no. 38)

Articulating the theological meaning of solidarity and naming it as a Christian virtue, John Paul II provided important insights for CST that are relevant to the USCCB's approach to peacebuilding.

Pope Francis on Solidarity and Hope

In the first papal TED Talk, in April 2017,[2] Pope Francis named solidarity as the foundation for hope in a world marked by individualism, consumerism, and waste. Recognizing our interdependence is key to overcoming a throwaway culture and directing technological and economic growth toward inclusion and equality. Francis also evokes solidarity in his social encyclical *Laudato si'* (2015) to emphasize responsibility toward future generations (*LS*, 162) and to argue for the preferential option for the poor (*LS*, 158).

The United States Conference of Catholic Bishops on Peacebuilding

This section discusses the USCCB's articulation of norms and principles for peacebuilding and the virtues and character of peacemakers and their contribution to the promotion of peace on multiple levels of society—not just in the face of war but also in people's everyday lives—in families, in the media, and so on.

---

2. Pope Francis, "Why the Only Future Worth Building Involves Everyone," TED Talk (April 2017), available at *https://www.ted.com/speakers/pope_francis*.

The Context of the United States Conference of Catholic Bishops' *The Challenge of Peace*

The theme of solidarity runs throughout the USCCB's pastoral letter *The Challenge of Peace: God's Promise and Our Response* (*CP*), in explicit and implicit ways, as the bishops stress human interdependence as the moral foundation for peace. The letter presents two approaches to peace within the Christian tradition—just war and nonviolence—as well as the USCCB's judgments on specific peace-related issues, especially nuclear weapons and the global arms race. The reality of modern warfare—with the potential to involve nuclear weapons and cause unprecedented destruction—created particular urgency for the bishops' message.

In addition to addressing specific issues related to modern warfare, the bishops spoke broadly about peace, articulating "a strong presumption against war" (*CP*, no. 70) and stressing that peace is more than the absence of war (*CP*, no. 68). Following the work of Pope John XXIII, the USCCB states: "Peace is both a gift of God and a human work. It must be constructed on the basis of central human values: truth, justice, freedom and love" (*CP*, no. 68).

The USCCB connects the pursuit of peace to the identity of a Christian, claiming that this pursuit is a necessary part of following Christ. It states, "The Christian has no choice but to defend peace, properly understood, against aggression. This is an inalienable obligation. It is the *how* of defending peace which offers moral options" (*CP*, no. 73). The bishops consider both the just war tradition and the tradition of nonviolence as morally acceptable approaches to achieving lasting peace and solidarity.

The Just War Tradition and Pacifism

The just war tradition offers guidelines for discerning when the use of force is morally legitimate, and it also offers principles for minimizing the harmful effects of war. The tradition of nonviolence or pacifism promotes peace with nonviolent means, opposing war and other forms of violence. Each of these traditions has a solid grounding in the Christian tradition and has developed historically as the Catholic Church has discerned how to live out the gospel mandate to seek the kingdom of God.

The traditions of just war and pacifism may strike some readers as contradictory. Pacifists claim that it is morally wrong to oppose violence with violence, while those who advocate for the just war tradition explain that violence is sometimes necessary in the defense of peace. The USCCB suggests that these approaches are not contradictory but are complementary ways to promote the ideal of peace in an imperfect world marked by violence. In their view, the Christian understanding of the kingdom of God in history grounds the Christian responsibility to build peace.

> Christians are called to live the tension between the vision of the reign of God and its concrete realization in history. The tension is often described in terms of "already but not-yet": i.e., we already live in the grace of the kingdom, but it is not yet the completed kingdom. . . . In the kingdom of God, peace and justice will be fully realized. Justice is always the foundation for peace. In history, efforts to pursue both peace and justice are at times in tension, and the struggle for justice may threaten certain forms of peace. (*CP*, nos. 58, 60)

In other words, the bishops recognize that Jesus' vision of the kingdom of God was marked by peace, making it the Christian ideal. At the same time, the kingdom of God is not fully present in history. It is something that Christians long for, work for, and pray for. In the messiness of human history, the world experiences injustices, such as genocide, widespread violence against women, and other atrocities. Recognizing this imperfect context, the question becomes, "How do Christians live into the kingdom of God in a world marked by injustices?"

Advocates of the just war theory do not rule out the use of force to address injustices. However, the just war tradition presumes a strong preference to avoid violence in the promotion of peace. The just war tradition emerged in the fifth century when Saint Augustine asked under what conditions Christians could use violence to defend Rome against invasion. Concluding that Christians could not be morally obligated to pursue pacifism at all costs, he began to develop guidelines for limiting the use of violence. The just war tradition, from the beginning, actively promoted peace.

The just war tradition seeks to minimize the harmful effects of war by outlining guidelines for discerning when it is just to go to war (*jus ad bellum*) and what strategies are just during times of war (*jus in bello*). The USCCB lists these principles in *Challenge of Peace* (see no. 85 ff.). The criteria for going to war include having a just cause, which does not include retribution. The bishops state that there must be a "real and certain danger" to innocent human life or human rights (*CP*, no. 86) in order to justify war. A just war also must follow the right intention, namely, the pursuit of peace against an imminent threat. A just war must also meet the criteria of being declared by a competent authority that wages war as a last resort after exhausting nonviolent alternatives. Finally, the moral acceptability of going to war is determined by the principles of comparative justice, proportionality, and the probability of success. In other words, the justice or good achieved by war must be worth the costs (*CP*, no. 99).

The main criteria for maintaining justice within war are proportionality and discrimination. The principle of proportionality requires tactics and strategies during war to be proportionate to the threat at hand. The principle of discrimination requires that the use of force be directed toward unjust aggressors, maintaining noncombatant immunity. The bishops note that the principles of proportionality and discrimination eliminate the legitimacy of total war, a war that would mean death for large numbers of innocent people (*CP*, no. 104). The bishops condemn such warfare, even to defend the innocent and most vulnerable. Specifically, they propose a preferential concern for the most vulnerable during times of war, stating, "It is of the utmost importance, in assessing harms and the justice of accepting them, to think about the poor and the helpless, for they are usually the ones who have the least to gain and the most to lose when war's violence touches their lives" (*CP*, no. 105).

Recognizing that all wars (just or unjust) threaten human life has led some people to adopt a pacifist approach to peacebuilding. The USCCB recognizes that God calls some Christians to manifest the ideal of the kingdom of God by adopting such an approach. Christian pacifists stress that peace is integral to Jesus' vision of the kingdom of God and that in his uncompromising dedication to the kingdom, Jesus demonstrated a commitment to nonviolence. In the Beatitudes, Jesus identifies peacemakers as the "children of God" (Matthew 5:9), naming nonviolence as a central commitment of Christian discipleship. Some Christian pacifists choose nonviolence because Jesus offered a nonviolent example in the face of a violent death on the cross.

Promoting Justice after War, Jus Post Bellum

Christian ethicists continually evaluate the appropriateness and applicability of the just war criteria. Stressing the importance of ongoing solidarity in the aftermath of war, some modern ethicists have suggested criteria for post-war justice or *jus post bellum*. Catholic social ethicists Mark Allman and Tobias Winright propose the following criteria: just cause (leave the affected area in a more just and stable condition than prior to war), reconciliation (take responsibility for wrongdoing, reinforcing accountability and forgiveness), punishment (exact any punishments with transparency, proportionality, and legitimate authority, often that of a third party), and restoration (address the economic, ecological, and social effects of the war).[3]

The USCCB praises the moral fortitude of individuals who follow Jesus' example of nonviolence and commit themselves to Christian pacifism, as witnesses to the kingdom of God. The bishops stress that Christian nonviolence is not passive but rather "affirms and exemplifies what it means to resist injustice through non-violent methods" (*CP*, no. 116). The bishops credit the nonviolent witness of well-known pacifist Mahatma Gandhi, an Indian Hindu, as well as Dorothy Day and Martin Luther King, for having a profound impact on the Catholic Church in the United States (*CP*, no. 117).

The bishops not only applaud individuals in history who have embraced nonviolence, but they also defend the right of an individual to resist participation in military combat if conscience dictates. Thus, the bishops argue for legal protection of conscientious objectors, those who oppose military service on the basis of their moral and religious

---

3. Mark J. Allman and Tobias L Winright, "When the Shooting Stops," *Christian Century* 127, no. 20 (October 2010): 26–29.

principles, as well as selective conscientious objectors, which refers to individuals who reject some but not all practices of military service (*CP*, no. 118). For example, a selective conscientious objector may be engaged in combat but refuse to use certain tactics that could endanger noncombatants, such as airstrikes. The bishops have continued to advocate for legal protection of conscientious objectors in the United States, where conscientious objection is granted as a privilege to individuals who meet strict conditions, but it is not considered to be a legal right.[4]

The USCCB refers to the Second Vatican Council to support the rights of conscientious objectors (*CP*, no. 118), quoting number 79 of *Gaudium et spes* (*Pastoral Constitution on the Church in the Modern World*, 1965), which explicitly addresses the rights of conscientious objectors: "Moreover, it seems right that laws make humane provisions for the case of those who for reasons of conscience refuse to bear arms." This statement is significant because before the council, the Catholic Church did not support conscientious objection. Less than ten years before Vatican II, in 1956, Pope Pius XII declared that conscientious objection to a lawful war was not an option for individuals: "a Catholic citizen cannot invoke . . . conscience in order to refuse to serve and fulfill those duties the law imposes."[5] The US bishops also

Daniel Berrigan, SJ (1921–2016), a well-known Catholic pacifist, drew upon the message of the gospel to oppose the Vietnam war and advocate for nuclear disarmament.

© Stephen Shames / Polaris / Newscom

---

4. Pax Christi USA, "Conscientious Objection and the Military," available at *http://paxchristiusa1.files.wordpress.com/2011/02/conscientious-objection-and-the-military-brochure.pdf*.

5. Pope Pius XII, "Christmas Radio Message" (December 23, 1956), in Harry Flannery, ed. *Pattern for Peace: Catholic Statements on International Order* (Westminster MD: Newman Press, 1962), 283.

rejected the legitimacy of conscientious objection throughout the first half of the twentieth century. Their position was consistent with the papal teaching of the time and was amplified by their interest in dispelling the widespread accusation that Roman Catholics were unpatriotic. Social ethicist Todd Whitmore describes how this influenced the bishops' public stance on conscientious objection: "Here, the issue of war arises not as a moral question about taking another person's life on behalf of the state but as a statement marking the boundaries, or the lack thereof, of American Catholic loyalty to the United States."[6] Today, US Catholics mirror the wider population in terms of their political commitments and expressions of patriotism.

The Harvest of Justice Is Sown in Peace

On the tenth anniversary of *The Challenge of Peace*, the USCCB revisited the relationship between pacifism and just war, publishing *The Harvest of Justice Is Sown in Peace* (*HJ*) in 1993. In it, the bishops reaffirm their support for pacifism and just war as moral options for the promotion of peace. Scholars note an important shift in the bishops' treatment of the role of collective acts of nonviolence. After the publication of *The Challenge of Peace* in 1983, the world witnessed nonviolent strategies that overcame and replaced totalitarian regimes in the Philippines and Eastern Europe. These movements illustrated the power of solidarity in overcoming injustice without the use of force. The bishops refer to these events saying,

> Although nonviolence has often been regarded as simply a personal option or vocation, recent history suggests that in some circumstances it can be an effective public undertaking as well. . . . One must ask, in light of recent history, whether nonviolence should be restricted to personal commitments or whether it also should have a place in the public order with the tradition of justified and limited war. (*HJ*, nos. 31, 33)

This marks a development from *The Challenge of Peace* when the bishops insisted that pacifism was an option for individuals and discussed

---

6. Todd Whitmore, "The Reception of Catholic Approaches to Peace and War in the United States," in *Modern Catholic Social Teaching: Commentaries and Interpretations*, ed. Kenneth Himes, et al. (Washington, DC: Georgetown University Press, 2005), 495.

it mainly within their defense of conscientious objection. In *The Harvest of Justice* the bishops took their commitment to nonviolence further, emphasizing nations' moral responsibility to explore the potential of effective nonviolence before resorting to violent conflict. The bishops also articulated this principle in *The Challenge of Peace;* however, between 1983 and 1993, the USCCB developed an enhanced appreciation for the proliferation of deadly weapons systems and the world witnessed effective nonviolent revolutions. These two developments led the bishops to become more skeptical about the use of force.

The bishops argue that the commitment to nonviolence must be fostered on both individual and collective levels. One of the ways that the bishops promote this is through reflecting on the spirituality of peacemaking. Spirituality, broadly speaking, refers to the way that an individual lives out his or her relationship with God. It touches on many aspects of one's faith life—prayer, religious devotions, and moral living. A spirituality of peacemaking allows people to develop practices that integrate the pursuit of peace into the way that they live out their faith. In *The Harvest of Justice*, the bishops connect Christian spirituality and peacemaking by encouraging all Christians to develop the virtues and vision of a peacemaker as an aspect of their faith life. Some of the virtues the bishops relate to the pursuit of peace are faith, hope, courage, compassion, kindness, and perseverance (*HJ*, no. 18).

Pax Christi USA

Pax Christi USA, affiliated with the multinational Catholic Pax Christi International, promotes peacebuilding through education and advocacy. Pax Christi USA works closely with Catholic parishes and bishops as well as other Christians to address specific threats to peace, including war, nuclear weapons, and violence. The organization emphasizes the need to promote peace on multiple levels—among nations and different communities in the United States, within families, and within one's own heart. Following this emphasis, they offer resources to connect Christian spirituality and peacebuilding. For more information, see their website at *https://paxchristiusa.org/*.

These virtues are rooted in and motivated by a particular vision of peace. The vision of peace that emerges from the insights of CST on solidarity can be achieved only through a commitment to the global common good. The USCCB summarizes this vision, drawing on the Catholic social tradition.

> [T]the Church's positive vision of a peaceful world includes: the primacy of the global common good for political life, the role of social and economic development in securing the conditions for a just and lasting peace, and the moral imperative of solidarity between affluent, industrial nations and poor, developing ones. (*HJ*, no. 21)

The principle of solidarity is central in this vision of peacemaking because it challenges unjust relationships that create the conditions of conflict. The bishops identify specific expressions of solidarity that strengthen the bonds of unity between nations. Solidarity involves promoting human rights across national, ethnic, religious, and cultural differences. Solidarity also demands international aid that supports human development and closes the extreme gap between wealthy and impoverished nations. The bishops advocate for institutions to promote these expressions of solidarity (*HJ*, no. 24). By emphasizing the importance of solidarity in peacebuilding, the bishops reinforce the connection between justice and peace.

Reading the Signs of the Times: Social Justice for US Veterans

War poses a number of ethical dilemmas, each of which demands careful analysis, reflection, and response. The most recent wars involving the United States, those in Iraq and Afghanistan, have caused thousands of military and civilian deaths. This section of the chapter will focus on the consequences of these wars for US veterans. This focus will provide a way to examine features of modern warfare and its consequences for military personnel. Drawing on the insights of US bishop and ethicist Robert McElroy, this section will analyze some of the implications of modern warfare in light of CST and the Catholic social tradition.

Army veteran Greg Valentini served multiple combat tours in Iraq and Afghanistan after enlisting in 2000. A decade later, Valentini was in the news as part of a class-action lawsuit filed by the ACLU of Southern California against the US Department of Veterans' Affairs. The lawsuit alleged that the VA had failed to leverage its resources to provide housing for the region's veterans. After returning from combat, Valentini struggled with Post Traumatic Stress Disorder (PTSD), drug addiction, and homelessness.[7] When the VA settled the lawsuit in 2015, the population of unhoused veterans was estimated to be 4,362. Since then, the population of unhoused veterans has declined in Los Angeles, but advocates point out the need for more stable housing, especially given the high cost of living in the area.[8]

The US Department of Veterans Affairs estimates between 11 and 20 percent of veterans who served in Iraq and 12 percent of veterans who served in Afghanistan, like Valentini, have experienced PTSD.[9] Some scholars estimate an even higher level of PTSD among veterans of these wars compared to previous wars. Factors contributing to high rates of PTSD include the type of fighting the soldiers have engaged in and the kind of preparation soldiers received. Wars like that carried out in Iraq, characterized by "urban street-fighting, civilian combatants and terrorism," may lead to an increased risk of PTSD among veterans.[10] Furthermore, 40 percent of the soldiers who have served in Iraq are members of the National Guard, with less military training than members of the regular forces, leaving them more vulnerable to PTSD.[11] Another source of PTSD,

---

7.Steve Lopez, "ACLU's lawsuit against the VA is a step in vet's recovery," *Los Angeles Times* (June 10, 2011), available at *http://articles.latimes.com/2011/jun/10/local /la-me-0609-lopez-vetlawsuit-20110609.*

8. In 2016, the unhoused veteran population was reported to be 3,071. Adam Nagourney, "Homelessness rises in Los Angeles, Except for Veterans and Families," *New York Times* (May 4, 2016), available *at https://www.nytimes.com/2016/05/05/us /los-angeles-homelessness-veterans-families.html.*

9. US Department of Veterans' Affairs National Center for PTSD, "How Common Is PTSD?" (updated Oct 2016), available at *https://www.ptsd.va.gov/public/ptsd -overview/basics/how-common-is-ptsd.asp.*

10. Peg Tyre, "Battling the Effects of War," *Newsweek* 144, no. 23 (December 6, 2004).

11. Ibid.

especially among women veterans, is sexual harassment or sexual assault in the military.[12]

The emotional, physical, and economic hardships that many US veterans face can go unnoticed by many Americans. Less than 1 percent of Americans have served in the Iraq and Afghanistan wars. One credible survey, for example, reported that 84 percent of Iraq and Afghanistan veterans think that the general US population fails to understand the struggles that military personnel and their families face.[13] The presence of a professional military and the elimination of the military draft allow many American voters and policy makers to remove themselves from the moral implications of warfare.

Given this reality, Bishop Robert McElroy concludes that, unlike previous eras of American history, "the United States has now achieved the capacity to wage major warfare over many years without greatly burdening its economy or general citizenry."[14] This context has allowed the United States to pursue the wars in Iraq and Afghanistan, both of which, McElroy suggests, lack a clear and attainable goal. Driven by the indefinite pursuit of societal transformation and the promotion of democracy, these wars led McElroy to suggest in 2011 that "the United States suffers from a paralyzing inability to bring wars to a close."[15] McElroy considers the war in Afghanistan to be "a moral hazard for the world and for the identity of the United States"[16] that continued without provoking widespread outrage because only a small percentage of US citizens who enter the military "absorb the terrible trauma of casualties in war."[17] In order to promote peace, McElroy argues all US citizens "must recognize that war inevitably brings horrendous unintended consequences."[18]

---

12. US Department of Veterans' Affairs National Center for PTSD, "How Common Is PTSD?" (updated Oct 2016), available at *https://www.ptsd.va.gov/public/ptsd -overview/basics/how-common-is-ptsd.asp.*

13. Pew Research Center, "War and Sacrifice in the Post 9/11 Era" (October 5, 2011), available at *http://www.pewsocialtrends.org/2011/10/05/war-and-sacrifice-in-the -post-911-era/.*

14. Robert McElroy, "War without End," *America* (February 21, 2011): 11.

15. Ibid., 12.

16. Ibid.

17. Ibid., 11.

18. Ibid., 13.

Rethinking Just War Theory

In 2016 the Vatican's Pontifical Council for Justice and Peace and Pax Christi International sponsored a conference on Non-violence and Just Peace. Leading thinkers and activists in the international Catholic peace movement came together to discuss experiences of nonviolence, the theological and biblical roots of Christian nonviolence, and the framework of "just peace," which emphasizes building right relationships as the foundation for peacebuilding. The participants concluded the conference with a written appeal to the Catholic Church to recommit to the centrality of gospel nonviolence. Specifically, they argued that the Church should no longer teach just war theory as an approach to Catholic peacebuilding.[19]

Summary and Integration for Service Learners

This chapter explored the ethical dimensions of war and the Catholic Church's ongoing struggle to promote peace in a world marked by violence. As articulated by the USCCB in *The Challenge of Peace*, Christians are called to be peacemakers, making it an important theme in Catholic social thought. The USCCB recognizes that for some, this involves an uncompromising commitment to nonviolence. Pacifists witness to the ideal of peace that the Church believes is a characteristic of the kingdom of God. For individuals who believe the demands of justice sometimes require the use of force, the just war theory provides ethical guidelines for ensuring that violent conflict is morally justified (*jus ad bellum*) and for minimizing the devastating effects of violence (*jus in bello*). The US bishops have recognized the

---

19. Catholic Nonviolence Initiative website, *https://nonviolencejustpeace.net/about/*. Arguing against just war theory, see Lisa Sowle Cahill, "A Church for Peace? Why Just War Theory Isn't Enough," in Commonweal (July 11, 2016), available at *https://www.commonwealmagazine.org/church-peace*. Arguing for a revised version of just war theory, see Mark Allman and Tobias Winright, *After the Smoke Clears: The Just War Tradition and Post War Justice* (Maryknoll, NY: Orbis Press, 2010).

legitimacy of pacifism and the just war approach but have noted that, as the destructive potential of modern warfare increases, the need for nonviolent solutions has become more urgent.

The principle of solidarity, as developed in the Catholic social tradition, provides a rationale for promoting peace through reinforcing just relationships between individuals and nations. By emphasizing human interdependence, solidarity calls us to lay the foundation for peace through promoting integral human development. Solidarity should also be fostered as a virtue, a habitual disposition or character trait that animates one's moral life. Framed in this way, peacemaking is a job not only for politicians and diplomats. Rather, everyone has the responsibility to become a peacemaker in daily life, recognizing human interconnectedness and responding justly.

Consider again your understanding of solidarity and peacemaking by revisiting the questions at the beginning of the chapter. Would you change any of your responses? What does solidarity mean to you now? What have you learned about violence and peace that might help you understand your own community and other communities? What might help you to better see or analyze a particular situation? How can the Catholic social tradition help you make judgments about unjust situations and determine the actions that promote justice in a particular context, including service-learning settings? Use the following vignette to practice the see-judge-act process.

See, Judge, Act in the Community

Vignette

As part of his service learning, one student participated in a recovery circle for people whose lives have been affected by substance abuse. During the hour, the student met Ben, a man in his mid-thirties who is currently homeless and struggling to overcome an addiction to alcohol. Listening to Ben's story, the student discovered that he began abusing alcohol after his tour of duty in Afghanistan to cope with feelings of anxiety. He had been diagnosed with PTSD but did not seek treatment because he did not want the alcohol abuse to be on his military record. Ben has been participating in a mentoring program with an older veteran who is helping him navigate some of the challenges of re-entering society after war.

See: Social Analysis

- What are some of the factors that may have led to Ben's experience of homelessness? How much of his situation can be attributed to his decisions and how much can be attributed to factors outside of his control—to other social, political, economic, or cultural realities?
- What information would you need to understand the impact of violence on Ben and the larger community?

Judge: Ethical Reflection

- Reflect on the vignette in light of Catholic social teaching and determine how you would apply the principle of solidarity to Ben's situation. Have breakdowns in solidarity likely contributed to his situation?
- How does Ben's situation factor into your understanding of the morality of war?

Act: Promoting Justice

- Based on what you have learned about CST and some of the ways violence impacts communities, what specific actions might be taken to promote peace? What structures, interests, or beliefs might hinder these proposed actions?
- What specific actions could be taken (by individuals, nations, and the international community) to reinforce solidarity?

Suggestions for Further Social Analysis in a Service-Learning Context

- Research different perspectives on how to define violence and then gather data on violence as it relates to a service-learning setting. What is the rate of violent crime in the community? How does it compare with surrounding neighborhoods? Has it gone up or down in recent history?
- Research theories on the effects of violence. Is a person's gender, age, religion, race, geographical location, or socioeconomic level a factor in the way violence affects her or him? Does violence affect some communities more than others? Explain. How do these theories contribute to the analysis

of the situations of people in a service-learning setting with which you are familiar?

- Investigate how a selected neighborhood or city addresses violence. What is the relationship of that community with its police? What community-led initiatives or nonprofit organizations are available to address violence in the community?

For Further Study on Catholic Social Thought and Peacebuilding

Printed Materials

Allman, Mark and Tobias Winright. *After the Smoke Clears: The Just War Tradition and Post War Justice.* Maryknoll, NY: Orbis Press, 2010.

Appleby, Scott, Robert Schreiter, and Gerard Powers, eds. *Peacebuilding: Catholic Theology, Ethics, and Praxis.* Maryknoll, NY: Orbis Press, 2010.

Fahey, Joseph. *War and the Christian Conscience: Where Do You Stand?* Maryknoll, NY: Orbis Press, 2005.

Love, Maryann Cusimano. "Building a Better Peace: A Future Worthy of our Faith." In *America* (July 21, 2015).

Massaro, Thomas and Thomas Shannon. *Catholic Perspectives on Peace and War.* Lanham, MD: Rowman & Littlefield, 2003.

McCarthy, Eli Sasaran. *Becoming Nonviolent Peacemakers: A Virtue Ethic for Catholic Social Teaching and U.S. Policy.* Eugene, OR: Wipf & Stock, 2012.

Whitmore, Todd. "The Reception of Catholic Approaches to Peace and War in the United States." In *Modern Catholic Social Teaching: Commentaries and Interpretations*, ed. Kenneth Himes, et al. Washington, DC: Georgetown University Press, 2005.

Websites

Pax Christi USA, *http://www.paxchristiusa.org/.*

Offers resources for education, prayer, and action related to nonviolence, overcoming racism, and conscientious objection.

7

CHAPTER

Care for Creation and Environmental Issues

Introduction

As evidence of global climate change grows and the availability of nonrenewable resources diminishes, more people are reflecting on their relationship to the natural world and searching for ways to promote responsibility toward the environment. Religious voices have emerged alongside secular ones on issues of environmental ethics. Christianity offers many resources for developing environmental ethics, including under the theological themes of stewardship, incarnation, and sacrament. Each of these theological themes has been important in developing an ethical response to the environment within the Catholic social tradition. Before learning about the Catholic Church's approach to environmental ethics, reflect on your understanding of humanity's relationship to the natural world.

- Is the proper treatment of the natural world a moral issue in your view? If so, when did it become so for you, and did your awareness develop over time? What are the beliefs, values, and priorities behind your position?

- What are some ways you or others in your community have been affected by the degradation of the environment? How does your community address environmental issues? What kinds of resources are available to people in your community who want to treat the environment responsibly?

- Consider the effects of environmental degradation on the people in a service-learning setting with which you are familiar.

How do these effects compare with those experienced by people in your immediate community? How does the community in which the service-learning setting is located address the abuse of the environment? What kinds of resources are available to people in that community who want to exercise responsibility for the environment?

- Do tensions exist between meeting fundamental human needs and caring for the environment? If so, do you notice differences in the ways various communities you are familiar with resolve these tensions? What might account for the differences?

This chapter will trace the development of Catholic social teaching's (CST) call for care for creation and will highlight how this principle guides responses to environmental issues. The theme is largely absent in the social encyclicals until the work of Pope Paul VI. Recent popes—John Paul II and Benedict XVI, and especially Francis—have made care for creation a priority in modern CST, issuing a strong critique of consumerism and individualism in their environmental ethic. Responding to this development, the United States Conference of Catholic Bishops (USCCB) has applied the principle of care for creation to concrete environmental problems, including global climate change. This chapter will also examine the teaching of Pope Francis and local Catholic leaders on the environment and conclude by drawing attention to the connection between racism and environmental degradation.

Before reading further, reflect on environmental problems and how consumerism and racism might influence them.

- Are consumerism and the condition of the environment related? What attitudes and institutions perpetuate consumerism? Who and what aspects of the natural world benefit from consumerism? Who and what aspects of the natural world are harmed by it?

- Do you observe a connection between racial discrimination and environmental degradation in your community or other communities you are familiar with through service learning? If so, what information would you need to determine if racism is a causal factor in this environmental degradation?

- How might a person's socioeconomic status affect the extent to which he or she is affected by problems in the environment?

This chapter will delve into the concept of stewardship of the earth as developed within CST by examining Pope Paul VI's *Octogesima adveniens* (*A Call to Action*) from 1971, when the growing awareness of moral issues in regard to the environment was relatively new. It will then look at the synod of bishops' statement, *Justice in the World,* also from 1971, that discusses the environment and its resources as part of globalization and the call for recognizing the interrelated nature of humanity. John Paul II and Benedict XVI continue the discussion of the disproportionate impact of environmental destruction on impoverished and marginalized communities in John Paul II's 1990 World Day of Peace message, *Peace with God the Creator, Peace with All of Creation,* and Benedict XVI's 2009 social encyclical, *Caritas in veritate* (*Charity in Truth*). Pope Francis demonstrates the inseparability of social justice and care for creation in his 2015 encyclical *Laudato si': On Care for Our Common Home.*

Lynn White's Challenge to Christianity

In 1967, historian Lynn White published an influential essay in which he argued that the Christian tradition was largely responsible for the current environmental crisis. He argued that two features of Christian belief were particularly detrimental to the development of Western thought: an anthropocentric (human-centered) view of the world and an instrumentalist view of nature, which understands the value of nature in terms of its usefulness to human beings.[1] His thought-provoking reading of Christian biblical and theological traditions has challenged many Christian ethicists and theologians to articulate a Christian response to the environmental crisis.

The chapter will also examine some ways the USCCB has focused on the principle of care for creation and the US bishops'

---

1. Lynn White Jr., "The Historical Roots of the Environmental Crisis," *Science* (1967): 1203–7.

application of the principle to specific ecological issues by exploring two letters issued by the bishops: *Renewing the Earth: An Invitation to Reflection and Action on Environment in Light of Catholic Social Teaching* (1991) and *Global Climate Change: A Plea for Dialogue, Prudence and the Common Good* (2001). The final section of the chapter provides a summary followed by a story of social change drawn from an actual service-learning setting and a series of questions designed to help readers practice aspects of the see-judge-act process.

Care for Creation in the Catholic Social Tradition

Early Catholic Social Teaching on the Environment

The early social encyclicals did not express concern about or develop teachings on the environment. This reflects broader cultural attitudes in the West in the late nineteenth and early twentieth centuries.

As the environmental movement began to develop in a secular context in the 1950s and 1960s, an environmental ethic emerged in the Catholic social tradition as well as in other faith traditions. The first Earth Day, in 1970, marked an important moment in the modern environmental movement because it gained widespread media attention and bipartisan political support that led to the creation of the United States Environmental Protection Agency.[2] The following year, Pope Paul VI noted in *Octogesima adveniens* (*A Call to Action*, 1971) the growing awareness of environmental degradation as a moral problem: "Man is suddenly becoming aware that by an ill-considered exploitation of nature he risks destroying it and becoming in his turn the victim of this degradation" (no. 21). By identifying environmental degradation as a new social problem, Paul VI places the principle of care for creation on the agenda of CST.

The 1971 synod of bishops took up issues of justice and continued the pope's concern for the consequences of human activity on the environment. The synod's statement, *Justice in the World* (*JW*), explicitly connects the pursuit of international solidarity with

---

2. For a history of Earth Day, visit the Earth Day Network's website at *https://www.earthday.org/*.

care for creation. The bishops observed that people throughout the world were becoming increasingly interconnected through advances in modern technology and the global economy. Because the earth's resources sustain human life, caring for them contributes to the common good and provides an impetus to develop global solidarity. The bishops note,

> Moreover, people are beginning to grasp a new and more radical dimension of unity; for they perceive that their resources, as well as the precious treasures of air and water—without which there cannot be life—and the small delicate biosphere of the whole complex of all life on earth, are not infinite, but on the contrary must be saved and preserved as a unique patrimony belonging to all human beings. (*JW*, no. 8)

Justice in the World articulates the relationship between care for creation and just international development by highlighting the relationship between economic inequality and environmental degradation. The synod critiques wealthy nations for overconsumption and excessive environmental pollution.

> [S]uch is the demand for resources and energy by the richer nations, whether capitalist or socialist, and such are the effects of dumping by them in the atmosphere and the sea that irreparable damage would be done to the essential elements of life on earth, such as air and water, if their high rates of consumption and pollution, which are constantly on the increase, were extended to the whole of humanity. (*JW*, no. 11)

The statements by Paul VI and the 1971 synod of bishops call people to be concerned for the environment and recognize environmental degradation as a moral issue. CST has continued since then to emphasize the link between caring for creation and insuring that all people are able to participate in the common good, a social reality that enables people to develop their God-given potential. The engagement of CST with environmental ethics was greatly enhanced by the work of Pope John Paul II, elected to the papacy in 1978, who drew on Catholic theological sources and ethical values to develop the principle of care for creation and to integrate it into the larger framework of CST. His successor, Pope Benedict XVI, continued that task.

Popes John Paul II and Benedict XVI on Care for Creation

Pope John Paul II integrated care for creation into CST by highlighting ways that environmental degradation harms people, especially those who are poor. John Paul II stressed ways that environmental destruction disproportionately impacts impoverished and marginalized communities in his 1990 World Day of Peace message, *Peace with God the Creator, Peace with All of Creation* (*PGC*). He argued that the environmental crisis is related to the injustices of poverty and war. He suggests that unjust land distribution and a lack of choices to promote sustainable farming can lead to uncontrolled deforestation. Modern warfare harms ecosystems on massive levels, polluting water and soil and destroying resources. The pope emphasized that addressing the ecological crisis requires a deep commitment to global solidarity, a commitment rooted in recognizing that the consumption patterns of industrialized nations are overburdening developing countries with environmental hazards. Within this perspective, global solidarity promotes peace and human development, which are essential for the adequate care for creation.

> When the ecological crisis is set within the broader context of *the search for peace* within society, we can understand better the importance of giving attention to what the earth and its atmosphere are telling us: namely, that there is an order in the universe which must be respected, and that the human person, endowed with the capability of choosing freely, has a grave responsibility to preserve this order for the well-being of future generations. I wish to repeat that *the ecological crisis is a moral issue.* (*PGC*, no. 15)

By naming the ecological crisis a moral issue, John Paul II reminded Catholics of "their serious obligation to care for all of creation" (*PGC*, no. 16).

One of the ways John Paul II challenged Catholics to carry out their moral obligation toward the environment is through resisting excessive materialism. In *Evangelium vitae* (*The Gospel of Life*, 1995), he argues that modern industrial societies suffer from an impoverished attitude toward life that is perpetuated by a consumer-driven culture that values *having* over *being*. Care for creation, from John Paul II's perspective, requires a cultural transformation that will eliminate extreme materialism and individualism characteristic of a consumer-driven culture. This transformation must be promoted through lifestyle changes that reflect a concern for the common good and a commitment to simplicity and moderation. He states,

> Modern society will find no solution to the ecological problem unless it *takes a serious look at its life style*. In many parts of the world society is given to instant gratification and consumerism while remaining indifferent to the damage which these cause. . . . If an appreciation of the value of the human person and of human life is lacking, we will also lose interest in others and in the earth itself. Simplicity, moderation and discipline, as well as the spirit of sacrifice, must become a part of everyday life, lest all suffer the negative consequences of the careless habits of a few. (*PGC*, no. 13)

Pope Benedict XVI continued the work of his predecessor, John Paul II, in many ways. In his 2009 social encyclical, *Caritas in veritate* (*Charity in Truth*), Benedict XVI identifies the connection between consumerism and the degradation of the environment (no. 51). Writing on the topic of human development in the midst of a global economic crisis, Benedict XVI's social encyclical critiques modern economic models that value efficiency and profit over the demands of solidarity. In this context, solidarity requires a more just distribution of resources among wealthy and impoverished nations, with a mindfulness of the needs of future generations. Specifically, in *Caritas in veritate* (*CV*), Benedict challenges wealthy industrialized nations to lower their energy consumption and look for alternative forms of renewable energy (no. 49). The logic of his environmental ethic lies in the pope's conviction that resources should be shared among all people because "the environment is God's gift to everyone" (*CV*, no. 48).

Green Initiatives at the Vatican

When it came to caring for the earth during his papacy, Pope Benedict XVI acted out his convictions in public ways. In 2007 he announced his intention to make Vatican City the first carbon neutral nation in the world. The Vatican started a tree farm in Hungary to absorb as much carbon dioxide as Vatican City produces each year. In addition, the Vatican has installed rooftop solar panels to reduce its use of nonrenewable energy.[3] Pope Francis has continued to advance green initiatives at the Vatican, most recently working with an electric car company to replace motorized vehicles in Vatican City.[4]

Benedict XVI, like John Paul II, approaches environmental ethics with particular attention to the human person. He has cautioned against approaches to the environment that deny the dignity of the human person and the legitimacy of human needs. At the same time, he argues,

> It is also necessary to reject the opposite position, which aims at total technical dominion over nature, because the natural environment is more than raw material to be manipulated at our pleasure; it is a wondrous work of the Creator containing a 'grammar' which sets forth ends and criteria for its wise use, not its reckless exploitation. (*CV*, no. 48)

For Benedict XVI the same natural law observable in the created world provides guidelines for how people should treat each other as well as how people should treat creation (*CV*, no. 51).

---

3. Elizabeth Rosenthal, "Vatican Penance: Forgive Us Our Carbon Output," *New York Times* (September 17, 2007).

4. Crux Staff, "Pope Francis Receives Electric Car as Part of Effort to Create 'Carbon Free' Vatican," (June 1, 2017), available at *https://cruxnow.com/vatican/2017/06/01/pope-francis-receives-electric-car-part-effort-create-carbon-free-vatican/*.

Pope Francis's Integral Ecology

On May 24, 2015, Pope Francis issued *Laudato si': On Care for Our Common Home,* the first major social encyclical on the environment. It takes its Latin title from a prayer attributed to St. Francis of Assisi, the patron saint of ecology and namesake of Francis's papacy. In the prayer, St. Francis gives thanks for all creatures, referring to the earth as his mother and the natural elements as brothers and sisters who glorify God by virtue of their creation. By integrating Franciscan spirituality throughout the encyclical, the pope urges all people to embrace their close connection to the natural world through a conversion of mind and heart.

Following his predecessors, the pope challenges readers to examine their own lifestyle and assume moral responsibility for the environment. He points to St. Francis, who adopted a life of radical simplicity and celebrated the intrinsic value of creation, as a model for how to respond to the ecological crisis. Furthermore, the pope insists that St. Francis "shows us just how inseparable the bond is between concern for nature, justice for the poor, commitment to society, and interior peace" (*LS*, no. 10). This statement reflects the pope's foundational conviction that environmental issues and social justice issues are inseparable.

Pope Francis draws upon Saint Francis of Assisi (d. 1226), the patron saint of ecology, in *Laudato si'*.

Francis's approach, summarized by the term *integral ecology*, begins with the observation that everything is interconnected. This view is echoed throughout the encyclical in a number of ways. Integral ecology invites people to understand themselves as part of nature, not separate from it. Francis reminds readers, "Human beings too are creatures of this world" (*LS*, 43). And while the pope maintains the unique dignity of human beings within creation, he also invites readers to humbly consider the entire created world as a family (*LS*, 89). Drawing upon the biblical and theological traditions of the Catholic Church, Francis rejects anthropocentric views that ignore the mystery of God reflected in the created world.

Seeking harmony between human beings and the rest of creation, Francis's integral ecology looks for solutions to environmental problems by examining their social, economic, cultural, and political dimensions. For example, the pope challenges pollution and waste by denouncing what he describes as a throwaway culture (*LS*, 22). Cultural attitudes that contribute to overconsumption and environmental degradation, the pope insists, are perpetuated by economic and political structures that measure development in terms of technological advancement and reward profit over solidarity.

Flowing from the conviction that everything is interconnected, integral ecology promotes the global common good and intergenerational solidarity. A theme also stressed by Benedict, intergenerational justice follows a shift in perspective, Francis insists. "Once we start to think about future generations, we look at things differently; we realize that the world is a gift which we have freely received and must share with others" (*LS*, 159). Following this perspective, Francis insists that the earth is our common home and specifically, "The climate is a common good, belonging to all and meant for all" (*LS*, 23).

Examining the reality of climate change allows the pope to illustrate the disproportionate impact of environmental degradation on marginalized communities and make a case for the preferential option for the poor. Although the warming of the earth is a global problem with numerous implications for everyone, Francis points out that impoverished countries and peoples are most impacted by its effects. For example, he argues the depletion of resources has the greatest impact on people who rely on fishing, forestry, and agriculture for sustenance (*LS*, 25). He also highlights the hardship of coastal communities who are forced to migrate because of rising sea levels (*LC*, 25). Against some critics, Pope Francis insists that climate change is rooted in human activity (*LC*, 23), and he challenges nations with economic and political power to tackle its root causes (*LC*, 26).

The pope argues at length that the ecological crisis is a moral issue. *Laudato si'* represents an important development in the Catholic social tradition as it highlights the environmental dimensions of social justice and integrates care for creation more concretely into the framework of Catholic social thought. Pope Francis, advocating for integral ecology, demonstrates how care for the earth promotes care for the poor and flows from a commitment to the global common good.

The United States Conference of Catholic Bishops on the Environment

This section will focus on the USCCB's teaching on the principle of care for creation and its application of this principle to specific ecological issues by exploring two letters: *Renewing the Earth: An Invitation to Reflection and Action on Environment in Light of Catholic Social Teaching* (1991) and *Global Climate Change: A Plea for Dialogue, Prudence and the Common Good* (2001). Regional bishops' conferences have addressed specific environmental issues by applying care for creation to their own contexts. This section will highlight one example—a statement by the bishops of the Northwest on the environmental issues surrounding the Columbia River watershed.

Renewing the Earth: Application of Catholic Social Teaching

Following Pope John Paul II's 1990 challenge to all Catholics to assume a moral responsibility for the environment, the USCCB issued a pastoral letter, *Renewing the Earth*. The bishops explain that the intent of the letter is to highlight the moral dimensions of the environmental crisis, particularly with respect to the poor and vulnerable, and to provide a religious perspective on ecological responsibility.

The bishops ground their position in CST. Specifically, in *Renewing the Earth* (no. 27) they list the following guidelines for their environmental ethic:

- *a God-centered and sacramental view of the universe*, which grounds human accountability for the fate of the earth;

- a consistent *respect for human life*, which extends to respect for all creation;
- a worldview affirming the ethical significance of *global interdependence and the common good;*
- *an ethic of solidarity* promoting cooperation and a just structure of sharing in the world community;
- an understanding of *the universal purpose of created things*, which requires equitable use of the earth's resources;
- *an option for the poor*, which gives passion to the quest for an equitable and sustainable world;
- a conception of *authentic development*, which offers a direction for progress that respects human dignity and the limits of material growth.

The first theme requires some elaboration as it provides the theological foundation for the bishops' position. A sacramental view of the universe presupposes that God is revealed through the created world. Catholic thought and practice emphasize the notion that the presence of God is mediated through tangible objects and rituals in a number of ways. This is exemplified in the seven sacraments the Catholic Church celebrates—baptism, confirmation, marriage, ordination, Eucharist, reconciliation, and anointing of the sick. Each of these rituals incorporates material elements and gestures to communicate a mystery of the Christian faith. The foundational belief behind the sacraments is that the physical world communicates God's invisible presence.

The bishops draw on the theological understanding of sacrament because experiencing God in the material aspect of the sacraments may also promote a reverence for all nonhuman creation, as it potentially reveals God's presence in the world. The bishops draw on the concept of sacrament to emphasize the value of creation by affirming the intrinsic value of nonhuman life. This provides a basis for care for creation. The bishops state in *Renewing the Earth* (*RE*), "The diversity of life manifests God's glory. . . . Accordingly, it is appropriate that we treat other creatures and the natural world not just as means to human fulfillment but also as God's creatures, possessing an independent value, worthy of respect and care" (no. 34).

The sacramental view of the world places God at the center of creation and has implications on how people should relate to the natural world. The bishops suggest, "Dwelling in the presence of God, we begin to experience ourselves as part of creation, as stewards within it, not separate from it" (*RE*, no. 31). They elaborate on their understanding of stewardship in the text. As stewards of creation, they argue, people are not free to use the earth's resources indiscriminately but should follow ethical guidelines for responsible management. Stewardship, they note, requires balancing human needs with the needs of the natural world.

The Meaning of Stewardship

A steward is entrusted with responsibility for something that belongs to a higher authority. Christians have used the concept of stewardship to emphasize responsibility toward creation out of recognition that it belongs to God. The concept has helped Christians interpret the Genesis account of Creation that instructs humans to have dominion over the earth (1:28). Environmentalists decry the effect of interpretations of this passage that suggest that people have unlimited authority over creation. Understanding the concept of *dominion* within the historical context of the Hebrew Bible, some scholars suggest that dominion has less to do with control and domination and more to do with establishing human connection to nature and mandating human responsibility toward it.[5] Even within this interpretation, environmentalists and ethicists within and outside of Christianity have critiqued the stewardship approach to ecology as not adequately demonstrating the interdependence of humanity and creation.[6]

---

5. For example, see Anne Clifford, "Foundations for a Catholic Ecological Theology of God," in *And God Saw That It Was Good: Catholic Theology and the Environment*, eds. Drew Christiansen and Walter Grazer (Washington, DC: USCCB, 1996), 22–28.

6. For example, see Elizabeth Johnson, *Women, Earth, and Creator Spirit* (New York: Paulist Press, 1993), who argues for a kinship model that expresses the relationship between human and nonhuman life in familial terms.

While affirming the value of nonhuman life, the USCCB does not let go of the unique dignity of the human person. The bishops do, however, recognize the potential tension between affirming the dignity of the human person and recognizing that humans exist within, not above, creation. The bishops invite Catholic theologians, Scripture scholars, and ethicists to "explore the relationship between this [the Catholic] tradition's emphasis on the dignity of the human person and our responsibility to care for all of God's creation" (*RE*, no. 71).

Renewing the Earth: Social Justice and the Environment

In *Renewing the Earth*, the USCCB highlights the relationship between social justice and care for creation. Specifically, they draw on the longstanding Catholic social principles of solidarity and the common good to frame human responsibility toward the environment. The bishops suggest that the ecological crisis presents an urgent opportunity to recognize "just how interdependent our world is" (*RE*, no. 36). Because all of humanity is affected by the abuse of the earth and overuse of the earth's resources, the environmental crisis transcends human divisions of culture, nationality, race, and ethnicity. At the same time, as the bishops have stressed, the environmental crisis affects groups in different ways. People in developing countries are harmed by environmental hazards and overconsumption of the earth's resources more than people living in other parts of the world. Solidarity, in the face of such disparity, becomes a foundational principle behind environmental justice because it invites Christians in wealthier nations to correct this disparity. The bishops argue that solidarity places particular demands on wealthy, industrialized countries like the United States, which might require "sacrifices of our own self-interest for the good of others and of the earth we share" (*RE*, no. 39).

A focal point of the bishops' work on the environment has been the intersection of ecological degradation, poverty, and racism. They explicitly point out the connection between the environment and economic justice:

The whole human race suffers as a result of environmental blight, and generations yet unborn will bear the cost for our failure to act today. But in most countries today, including our own, it is the poor and the powerless who most directly bear the burden of current environmental carelessness. Their lands and neighborhoods are more likely to be polluted or to host toxic waste dumps, their water to be undrinkable, their children to be harmed. Too often, the structure of sacrifice involved in environmental remedies seems to exact a high price from the poor and from workers. (*RE*, no. 7)

By focusing on the human dimension of the environmental crisis—how it diminishes human life and perpetuates inequalities between the rich and the poor—the bishops are able to make solid connections between the care for creation and other principles of CST. In particular, the USCCB's discussion of environmental ethics consistently reflects the Catholic Church's commitment to human dignity, the common good, and the option for the poor.

Promoting environmental justice relates to the Catholic Church's defense of the poor and vision of authentic human development. The bishops refer to the foundational work of Pope Paul VI, stressing that the Catholic Church considers human development not only in terms of economic growth but also the social, spiritual, and moral development of a person. The bishops state, "Catholic social teaching has never accepted material growth as a model of development. . . . Authentic development supports moderation and even austerity in the use of material resources" (*RE*, nos. 45, 46). This understanding of development is conducive to promoting balance between economic growth and care for creation. Within the vision of development offered by Catholic social thought, the accumulation of material goods is not the sole indicator of human flourishing. Rather, integral development relates to the cultural, moral, and spiritual well-being of a person and community.

Global Climate Change

In recent years, the USCCB has been vocal about the need for an immediate response to a specific environmental concern—climate change. The bishops point to a growing consensus in the scientific community that Earth's temperatures are changing at an alarming rate, causing a number of environmental hazards, such as floods, coastal erosion, and loss of biodiversity. Scientists understand the primary cause of this rapid change to be carbon emissions from human activities: industry, transportation, and deforestation.[7] The issue of climate change has become contentious within the United States, with political debates on the threat of global climate change and the ways to address it.[8] In their 2001 statement *Global Climate Change: A Plea for Dialogue, Prudence and the Common Good* (*GCC*), the USCCB focuses the reader's attention beyond the political debates to the moral issue of environmental responsibility.

> At its core, global climate change is not about economic theory or political platforms, nor about partisan advantage or interest group pressures. It is about the future of God's creation and the one human family. It is about protecting both "the human environment" and the natural environment. It is about our human stewardship of God's creation and our responsibility to those who come after us. (*GCC*, no. 3)

In the text, the bishops draw on CST to address the issue of climate change, appealing to the common good and an ethic of solidarity. The bishops challenge environmentalists who identify overpopulation in developing countries as a central cause of global climate change. The bishops invite the reader to focus, instead, on the problems of materialism and consumption in developed countries.

> The global climate change debate cannot become just another opportunity for some groups—usually affluent advocates from the developed nations—to blame the problem on population growth in poor countries. Historically, the industrialized countries have emitted more greenhouse gases that warm the climate than have the developing countries. Affluent nations such as our own have to acknowledge the impact of voracious consumerism instead of simply calling for population and emission controls from people in poorer nations. (*GCC*, no. 22)

---

7. See the Center for Climate and Energy Solutions's website.

8. For information on the public debates, see Andrew Hoffman, *How Culture Shapes the Climate Change Debate* (Stanford: Stanford University Press, 2015).

The USCCB's emphasis on curbing consumption rather than population control reflects the teachings of Popes John Paul II and Benedict XVI on the environment.

The Bishops of the Northwest on the Columbia River Watershed

Unlike climate change, which impacts the entire globe, some environmental issues are specific to particular regions and require a more local response. Regional groups of bishops have addressed such issues in the United States. The bishops of New England, New Mexico, Alaska, and Florida have made statements on specific environmental issues impacting their churches. One of the best examples of collaboration among regional bishops can be observed in the statement on the Columbia River watershed.

Building on principles laid out in *Renewing the Earth*, a group of bishops from the Pacific Northwest[9] wrote a pastoral letter in 2000 on the ethical dimensions surrounding the Columbia River watershed. Specifically, they raise concern about the impact of logging, mining, and fishing on the watershed's ecosystem. At the same time, they recognize how important these industries are to local residents. In their letter, they reflect on the challenge of balancing human needs with proper care for the earth. They begin their reflection by stating that "the watershed is ultimately God's; human beings are entrusted with responsibility for it, concern for its species and ecology, and regulation of its competitive and complementary uses."[10] The writers recognize that industries such as fishing, logging, and mining have been important sources of livelihood to the residents of the Northwest, and they also recognize that these industries have contributed to ecological damage in the area. For this reason, the bishops acknowledge the tensions that emerge between landowners, workers, and environmental groups. Observing this tension, the bishops call for "a thorough, humble and introspective evaluation that seeks to

---

9. This includes bishops from Washington, Oregon, Montana, Idaho, and British Columbia.

10. Columbia River Pastoral Letter Project, "The Columbia River Watershed: Caring for Creation and the Common Good" (2000), available at *http://www.thewscc.org/uploads/3/4/9/4/34945816/crplp.pdf.*

eliminate both economic greed that fails to respect the environment, and ecological elitism that lacks a proper regard for the legitimate rights and property of others."[11]

The northwestern bishops highlight a prominent theme in CST on the environment in their concern for human needs in relation to the environment. The Columbia River watershed provides just one example of how resource management and conservation can exist in tension with people's jobs and interests. In response, the bishops invite dialogue on how to balance the immediate interests and needs of people with long-term planning on care for the environment.

Reading the Signs of the Times: Environmental Racism

This section will further discuss the disproportionate impact of environmental harm on racial minorities. Identified as environmental racism, this is a significant moral issue in the United States today.

In 2015 Dr. Mona Hanna-Attisha, a pediatrician in Flint, Michigan, began documenting elevated lead levels in her young patients. As a pediatrician, she knew the dangers of lead exposure, especially among children under age six. The American Academy of Pediatrics considers no level of lead exposure to be safe for children and points out how even small amounts of lead can negatively impact a child's brain development, growth, and overall health.[12] Dr. Hanna-Attisha became concerned about her patients after observing frequent rashes and hearing their complaints of brown, smelly water in their homes.

In 2014, the state of Michigan had switched Flint's water supply from Lake Huron to the Flint River. Suspecting inadequate corrosion controls, researchers had already confirmed that the water supply in Flint contained unsafe levels of lead as defined by the Environmental Protection Agency (EPA).[13] Despite concerns voiced by the

---

11. Ibid., 2.

12. American Academy of Pediatrics "Lead Exposure in Children," available at *https://www.aap.org/en-us/advocacy-and-policy/aap-health-initiatives/lead-exposure /Pages/Lead-Exposure-in-Children.aspx.*

13. Jim Lynch, "EPA Stayed Silent on Flint's Tainted Water," *Detroit News* (January 12, 2016), available at *http://www.detroitnews.com/story/news/politics/2016/01/12 /epa-stayed-silent-flints-tainted-water/78719620/.*

researchers and local residents, the state's Department of Environmental Quality (DEQ) did not advise local residents to protect themselves. Hanna-Attisha's research compared her patients' lead levels to children before the 2014 switch in the city's water supply and found that lead levels had doubled and, in some neighborhoods, tripled. Although the state initially challenged her findings, her research was later acknowledged as correct and the director of the DEQ and state governor admitted they were wrong in addressing the issue.[14]

Some activists have cited the Flint water crisis as evidence of environmental racism, pointing out that the majority of Flint's residents are black and 40 percent live below the poverty line.[15] Environmental racism names a connection between institutionalized discrimination and the degradation of the environment. Sociologist Robert Bullard suggests, "environmental racism refers to environmental policies, practices, or directives that differentially affect or disadvantage (whether intentionally or unintentionally) individuals, groups, or communities based on race or color."[16] Environmental racism is perpetuated by social structures and attitudes that discriminate against racial minorities.

Even when environmental regulations are in place, communities may experience different levels of enforcement of those protections. Studies have shown that people of color and low-income communities in the United States experience less environmental protection than majority white communities. Industries dispose of more waste and emit more toxins near predominantly minority communities than near predominantly white communities, which tend to have more economic and political power.[17]

The reality of environmental racism demonstrates the connection between social justice and environmental justice, a theme that

---

14. Holly Yan, "Flint Water Crisis: How Years of Problems Led to Lead Poisoning," CNN (March 28, 2017).

15. Steve Almasy and Laura Ly, "Flint Water Crisis: Report Says 'Systemic Racism' Played Role," CNN (February 18, 2017), available at *http://www.cnn.com/2017/02/18/politics/flint-water-report-systemic-racism/index.html*.

16. Robert Bullard, "Confronting Environmental Racism in the Twenty-First Century," *Global Dialogue* 4, no. 1 (Winter 2002): 2.

17. Robert Bullard, Paul Mohai, Robin Saha, and Beverly Wright, "Toxic Wastes and Race at Twenty," *Environmental Law* 38, no. 2 (Spring 2008): 371–411.

is strongly developed in Catholic social thought since the late 1970s. Walter Grazer, writing as the director of the USCCB's Environmental Justice Program, identifies the integration of social justice and care for creation as a primary challenge for the Catholic Church. According to Grazer, such integration requires listening to marginalized voices. "We must find a way to give expression to the voices, needs and hurts of the poor and vulnerable if we are to integrate the search for social justice and environmental wholeness."[18] He goes on to identify specific ways that the US Catholic community is making an effort to place the needs of people living in poverty at the center of environmental justice programs. For example, Catholic Charities USA trains low-income families to avoid exposure to household toxins and the Catholic Campaign for Human Development advocates for farmers who are exposed to harmful pesticides on the job.[19]

Summary and Integration for Service Learners

The Catholic Church's teaching on care for creation reveals a concern for how environmental destruction affects human life, particularly the lives of the most vulnerable. For Popes Francis, John Paul II, and Benedict XVI, the care for creation is understood in light of other Catholic social principles, particularly solidarity, the common good, and human dignity. Their teachings challenge wealthy individuals and nations to consider the effect of overconsumption on people and nations suffering from poverty. This option for the poor and vulnerable is a central principle underlying the Catholic Church's teachings about the need to bring justice to people suffering from environmental racism.

The USCCB links social justice with their approach to the environment, emphasizing the human suffering caused by environmental destruction. They have articulated the intrinsic value of creation and have invited Catholics to practice care for the environment as an aspect of their faith. The current challenge for CST on the environment was

---

18. Walter Grazer, "Environmental Justice: A Catholic Voice," *America* 190, no. 2 (January 19, 2004): 15.

19. Ibid., 13.

summarized in the USCCB's invitation to theologians, biblical scholars, and ethicists to continue to reflect on the relationship between human dignity and care for creation (*RE*, no. 71).

Now that you have read about the principle of care for creation articulated in CST, revisit your responses to the questions at the beginning of the chapter. Would you answer any questions differently? Does the chapter's discussion about environmental degradation and its connection to racism shed light on social issues you've encountered in a service-learning setting? Use the following vignette and questions to practice aspects of the see-judge-act process in relation to this topic.

See, Judge, Act in the Community

Vignette

As a faculty member, Dave sought community partners that would provide a context for students to learn about social inequalities and how communities promote social change. At first, he was skeptical about partnering with a community garden, doubting its potential to teach students about such social issues. During an orientation, however, he learned that the location of the garden, situated in a predominantly African American low-income neighborhood, had previously been a site of illegal dumping and drug activity. The neighbors had planted a garden as a way to "take back their block," get to know their neighbors, and promote health and wellness through nutrition. The resident-led initiative expanded beyond a garden to include block events and outdoor art installations, transforming the block and perceptions about the neighborhood.

See: Social Analysis

- What information would help you assess the extent to which racial discrimination may have contributed to illegal dumping on the block?

- How does social change happen in the situation illustrated in the vignette? Does the community garden initiative address structural inequalities? How did the initiative challenge the professor's initial assumptions about social justice?

Judge: Ethical Reflection

- How might the Catholic social principles of subsidiarity and solidarity apply to the situation described in the vignette?
- How does Pope Francis's invitation to consider the relationship between the unique dignity of the person and care for creation relate to the situation addressed by the community partner?

Act: Promoting Justice

- Identify actions aligned with CST's calls to care for creation and protect the dignity of human beings that might help to prevent environmental racism.
- Identify any attitudes, policies, and institutions that you are aware of that, according to CST, should be challenged in order to address disparities in the enforcement of environmental protections.

Suggestions for Further Social Analysis in a Service-Learning Context

- Gather data on environmental hazards and the racial and socioeconomic demographics in three or more neighborhoods or communities in a selected city. Does the data suggest any correlation between the number and types of hazards and the race or socioeconomic status of the people in the neighborhoods?
- Research the debates about global climate change. How do the various positions you encounter relate to environmental policies?
- Investigate the availability of green lifestyle options (e.g., recycling, composting, organic and biodegradable products, sustainable energy sources) in a selected neighborhood or city. Compare these findings with the availability of such options in other areas. If you find differences, consider what might contribute to them.

For Further Study on Catholic Social Thought on the Environment

Printed Materials

Christiansen, Drew, and Walter Grazer, eds. *And God Saw That It Was Good: Catholic Theology and the Environment*. Washington, DC: USCCB, 1996.

Cloutier, David. *Walking God's Earth: The Environment and Catholic Faith*. Collegeville, MN: Liturgical Press, 2014.

DiLeo, Daniel R., ed. *All Creation Is Connected: Voices in Response to Pope Francis's Encyclical on Ecology*. Winona, MN: Anselm Academic, 2017.

Miller, Richard, ed. *God, Creation, and Climate Change: A Catholic Response to the Environmental Crisis*. Maryknoll, NY: Orbis, 2010.

Nothwehr, Dawn. *Ecological Footprints: An Essential Franciscan Guide for Faith and Sustainable Living*. Collegeville, MN: Liturgical Press, 2012.

Schaefer, Jame. *Confronting the Climate Crisis: Catholic Theological Perspectives*. Milwaukee: Marquette University Press, 2011.

Taylor, Sarah McFarland. *Green Sisters: A Spiritual Ecology*. Cambridge, MA: Harvard University Press, 2009.

Winright, Tobias, ed. *Green Discipleship: Catholic Theological Ethics and the Environment*. Winona, MN: Anselm Academic, 2011.

Websites

Catholic Climate Covenant, *http://www.catholicclimatecovenant.org/*.

Provides videos and written materials on climate change and environmental justice. Offers resources for assessing and reducing one's carbon footprint and invites people to take the "St. Francis Pledge" to care for the planet.

Rights and Responsibilities in a Globalized Context

Introduction

The Catholic social tradition affirms that the dignity of human persons can be safeguarded only if the rights of individuals are protected. Demonstrating a strong commitment to the common good, the Catholic Church has promoted a distinctive approach to human rights that affirms the social nature of the person and the importance of solidarity. For this reason, Catholic social teaching (CST) discusses rights alongside responsibilities. The principle of rights and responsibilities communicates a foundational commitment of the Catholic social tradition—to protect the dignity of the individual and the good of a community at the same time. Reflect on your understanding of human rights and responsibilities and, if possible, relate this understanding to service-learning settings with which you may be familiar.

- What is the meaning of *human rights*? What rights are universal? What experiences, ideas, and values have shaped your understanding of human rights?
- How do you understand your responsibility to the communities with which you identify most immediately (family, neighborhood, university) and then more broadly (city, nation, world)? How do you understand your responsibility to communities you may be familiar with through service learning?
- How are rights to private property, health care, and education protected within the context of a service-learning setting with

which you are familiar and within the broader community where that setting is located? Does everyone have access to these resources and to the same extent? If not, what limits a person's access to these resources?

The protection of human rights and the carrying out of responsibilities are affected by globalization, which describes multiple features of the contemporary world. Sociologists David Held and Andrew McGrew offer a helpful definition: "globalization denotes the expanding scale, growing magnitude, speeding up and deepening impact of interregional flows and patterns of social interaction."[1]

There are many economic, political, and cultural implications of globalization that raise ethical questions. This chapter focuses on economic globalization, which is characterized by the flow of goods, services, and technology across borders and the interdependence among national economies. Consider the meaning and significance of economic globalization and, if possible, relate these ideas to a service-learning setting with which you are familiar.

- What are some benefits of economic globalization? What are some of its harmful effects? Have you experienced any of the benefits or harms? Has economic globalization affected anyone you may have met through service learning? If so, how?

- Who are the major actors behind economic globalization? Do certain groups of people tend to hold power that helps to direct globalization? If so, who, and what is the source of their power? What social structures would need to be analyzed to understand better the power dynamics behind globalization?

- Identify local organizations that work to meet the needs of the poor, and consider how their efforts relate to globalization. Do these efforts suggest some specific ways that local initiatives can contribute to worldwide change?

This chapter will explore the development of the principle of rights and responsibilities in CST and examine how the United States

---

1. David Held and Andrew McGrew, "The Great Globalization Debate," in *The Global Transformations Reader: An Introduction to the Globalization Debate*, eds. David Held and Andrew McGrew (Malden MA: Blackwell/Polity Press, 2004), 4.

Conference of Catholic Bishops (USCCB) has applied this principle in response to issues raised by economic globalization, focusing on two of their statements, *Called to Global Solidarity: International Challenges for US Parishes* (1997) and *A Place at the Table* (2002). It will also highlight how the bishops have implemented these teachings through the work of Catholic Relief Services and the Catholics Confront Global Poverty campaign. Next, the chapter will draw on insights from Christian ethics to help service learners begin to analyze globalization and assess its effects. The final section of the chapter provides a summary followed by a vignette drawn from an actual service-learning setting and a series of questions designed to help readers become more familiar with the see-judge-act process.

Catholic Social Teaching on Rights and Responsibilities

Rights and Duties in the Early Social Encyclicals

The Catholic Church's position on human rights has developed over time and is best understood within the context out of which it emerged. In 1864, Pope Pius IX issued a *Syllabus of Errors*, in which he explicitly rejected characteristic features of modernity, including the right to religious liberty and the right to freedom of speech.[2] The pope associated these rights with modernity, the Enlightenment, and the French Revolution, all of which he considered threats to the Catholic Church's authority. The pope and many of his contemporaries feared that the Enlightenment's emphasis on human reason and individual freedoms were incompatible with the Church's emphasis on the social nature of the person, the authority of the Church, and the objectivity of moral truth. This reactionary approach to the Western tradition of human rights influenced Catholic thought until the Second Vatican Council.

The early social encyclicals (1891–1931) of Popes Leo XIII and Pius XI moved beyond Pius IX's rigid condemnation of modernity. Both popes defended the natural right to private property in

---

2. Pope Pius IX, *Quanta Cura and the Syllabus of Errors* (1864), nos. 15, 79 (Kansas City: Angelus Press, 1998).

an effort to argue against socialism. They also argued that a person's right to private property is not absolute: it is limited by the person's duty or responsibility to promote the common good. By emphasizing duties alongside rights, the early social encyclicals rejected what they saw as the dangers of Enlightenment thinking—individualism and unlimited freedom—without rejecting all features of modernity.

Pope John XXIII and the Catholic Human Rights Tradition

Pope John XXIII was instrumental in integrating the discussion of specific human rights into the Catholic Church's official social teaching. He articulated a vision of human rights in his social encyclical *Pacem in terris* (*Peace on Earth*, 1963),[3] an encyclical that made a significant contribution to the Catholic human rights tradition. Social ethicist David Hollenbach argues that "*Pacem in terris* moved the leadership of the Church from a position of staunch opposition to modern rights and freedoms to activist engagement in the global struggle for human rights. This shift was one of the most dramatic reversals in the long history of the Catholic tradition."[4]

Pacem in terris (*PT*) was the first major papal writing to be addressed to the whole world, not just Catholics. The universal audience of the encyclical reflects the universal scope of its content. John XXIII articulated an awareness of the growing interdependence of people throughout the world and argued for universal human rights out of the recognition of that interdependence. The pope expressed his support for the United Nations' 1948 *Universal Declaration of Human Rights* (*PT*, nos. 143–44) and echoed many of the declaration's themes.

John XXIII grounds his argument for universal human rights in natural law, appealing to an understanding of human nature reflected in Catholic teaching. He begins with the conviction,

---

3. Drew Christiansen, "Commentary on *Pacem in Terris* (Peace on Earth)," in *Modern Catholic Social Teaching*, eds. Himes, et al. (Washington, DC: Georgetown University Press, 2005), 224.

4. David Hollenbach, "Commentary on *Gaudium et Spes*," in *Modern Catholic Social Teaching*, eds. Himes, et al. (Washington, DC: Georgetown University Press, 2005), 280.

> Any well-regulated and productive association of men in society demands the acceptance of one fundamental principle: that each individual man is truly a person. His is a nature, that is, endowed with intelligence and free will. As such he has rights and duties, which together flow as a direct consequence from his nature. (*PT*, no. 9)

John XXIII offers a person-centered understanding of rights, emphasizing the dignity of the human person rooted in the human qualities of rationality and free will. Within this perspective, rights and responsibilities flow from human existence and not from specific actions or ideas. Grounded in human dignity, human rights are intrinsic and universal, not earned or granted to a person based on certain conditions.

Continuing the Catholic social tradition's emphasis on the call to community and the common good, John XXIII describes human rights as protected by social life. The rights listed in *Pacem in terris* include the basic necessities for human life such as food, shelter, and medical care, as well as rights that enable people to participate fully in the life of a society—education, participation in political life, and freedom to worship God according to one's conscience. Affirming that rights are always realized in the context of community, John XXIII lists individual rights, along with corresponding duties to support the rights of others and protect the common good. For example, the right to life involves the duty to preserve life; the right to freedom of conscience carries the duty to seek the truth (*PT*, no. 9).

Popes Paul VI and John Paul II: Solidarity and Human Rights

Papal teaching after Vatican II reflects a strong commitment to human rights and consistently speaks about these rights in connection with responsibilities toward the community. In *Populorum progressio* (*The Development of Peoples*, 1967), Pope Paul VI emphasized the relationship between rights and responsibilities. In *Populorum progressio* (*PP*), he expresses his views on private property: "The right to private property is not absolute or unconditional. No one may appropriate surplus goods solely for his own private use when others lack the bare necessities of life" (no. 23). Paul VI continues the Catholic social tradition's insistence on the universal purpose of created things to stress that the right to private property is a limited right. Writing with an awareness of severe economic inequalities, Paul VI argued that responsibility for the common good sets limits on a person's right to accumulate wealth. For example, the pope criticizes wealthy individuals who hoard their money through foreign investments rather than giving back to their local community (*PP*, no. 24). In the face of growing inequalities between nations, Paul VI calls wealthier countries to solidarity with developing countries.

In his 1987 social encyclical *Sollicitudo rei socialis* (*On Social Concern*), Pope John Paul II follows Paul VI's call for solidarity in response to the increasingly inequitable distribution of resources throughout the world. In *Sollicitudo rei socialis* (*SRS*), he argues for just distribution of goods out of a spirit of international solidarity.

> It is necessary to state once more the characteristic principle of Christian social doctrine: the goods of this world are originally meant for all. The right to private property is valid and necessary, but it does not nullify the value of this principle. Private property, in fact, is under a "social mortgage," which means that it has an intrinsically social function, based on and justified precisely by the principle of the universal destination of goods. (no. 42)

John Paul II highlights the meaning of rights and responsibilities in his understanding of private property. Because creation is intended for the benefit of all, one cannot legitimately hoard a surplus of goods while others are lacking basic necessities. The pope observes an unjust distribution of goods in the international community and identifies some specific problems with the global economy that perpetuate such injustice. He argues that international trade systems disadvantage developing countries by devaluing their raw materials. He also notes that multinational companies take advantage of low-cost labor in some countries without ensuring fair labor laws (*SRS*, no. 43). The pope invites a reexamination of international systems that regulate finance and exchange, arguing that they have failed to promote the development of all nations

(*SRS*, no. 43). He proposes collaboration among nations to secure the rights of everyone.

Pope Benedict XVI and Pope Francis on Globalization and Human Rights

In his 2009 message for World Peace Day, Pope Benedict XVI addressed the challenge of ameliorating human rights violations and injustices, which contribute to the marginalization of the poor throughout the world.

> Globalization eliminates certain barriers, but is still able to build new ones; it brings peoples together, but spatial and temporal proximity does not of itself create the conditions for true communion and authentic peace. Effective means to redress the marginalization of the world's poor through globalization will only be found if people everywhere feel personally outraged by the injustices in the world and by the concomitant violations of human rights.[5]

In his social encyclical *Caritas in veritate* (*Charity in Truth*, 2009), Benedict XVI offers a strong critique of the trends in economic globalization that trample the rights of the poor. In *Caritas in veritate* (*CV*), Benedict XVI argues for a global ethic based on the virtue of gratuitousness, through which all people would recognize the goods of creation as gifts to be shared. The notion of gratuitousness counteracts current driving forces of the market—consumerism and competition. Benedict XVI argues that gratuitousness fosters solidarity, and that solidarity is badly needed in a globalized economy that too often suppresses the poor (*CV*, nos. 34–35).

Benedict XVI also makes the point that "the economic sphere is neither ethically neutral, nor inherently inhuman and opposed to society. It is part and parcel of human activity and precisely because it is human, it must be structured and governed in an ethical manner" (*CV*, no. 36). Benedict XVI regards globalization in a similar way—it

---

5. Pope Benedict XVI, "Fighting Poverty to Build Peace," Message on the 2009 World Day of Peace, no. 8, available at *http://www.vatican.va/holy_father/benedict_xvi /messages/peace/documents/hf_ben-xvi_mes_20081208_xlii-world-day-peace_en.html.*

is not inherently good or bad but should be directed to the service of humanity. He states,

> As a human reality, it [globalization] is the product of diverse cultural tendencies, which need to be subjected to a process of discernment. The truth of globalization as a process and its fundamental ethical criterion are given by the unity of the human family and its development towards what is good. Hence a sustained commitment is needed so as to *promote a person-based and community-oriented cultural process of world-wide integration that is open to transcendence.* (*CV*, no. 42)

Emphasizing the unity of the human family, the pope stresses the importance of solidarity in directing the process of economic globalization. The principle of rights and responsibilities can also be seen throughout the text. The pope argues that an individual's economic rights carry responsibilities toward the flourishing of the whole community. As the world's inhabitants become increasingly interconnected through the process of globalization, human flourishing takes on a global dimension. In order to direct economic globalization toward human flourishing, Benedict XVI argues for cooperation between nations as well as the establishment of an international authority to ensure democratic oversight of the global economy (*CV*, no. 41).

Echoing Benedict, Francis calls for "cooperative globalization" that promotes solidarity and the flourishing of all people.[6] Francis is particularly concerned that economic globalization has a "levelling effect on cultures" (*LS*, no. 144) by importing the values of a free-market economy—individualism, a "consumerist vision of human beings," and apathy toward suffering (*EG*, no. 54). He argues, "In many countries globalization has meant a hastened deterioration of their own cultural roots and the invasion of ways of thinking and acting proper to other cultures which are economically advanced but ethically debilitated" (*EG*, no. 62).

---

6. Devin Sean Watkins, "Pope's term 'cooperative globalization' call to rethink economic responsibility," Vatican Radio (January 26, 2017), available at *http://en.radio vaticana.va/news/2017/01/26/popes_term_cooperative_globalization/1288370.*

The Vatican Calls for Corporate Responsibility

In 2012, the Pontifical Council for Justice and Peace issued a statement entitled, "The Vocation of the Business Leader: A Reflection." The reflection is presented as a resource to help business leaders connect their work to Christian values. Following the model of *see-judge-act*, the text invites business leaders to (1) observe the challenges and opportunities for promoting economic justice through their work, (2) judge their observations in light of the principles of human dignity and the common good, and (3) act on behalf of justice in their vocation, connecting their faith to their career in business leadership.[7]

The United States Conference of Catholic Bishops on Global Responsibility

This section will examine how the USCCB has applied the principle of rights and responsibilities to frame the US role in the international community. The work of protecting human rights and meeting responsibilities for the common good presents particular challenges and opportunities for those living in the United States. US culture, with its strong emphasis on personal freedom and the opportunity to accumulate wealth, does not readily support the notion of responsibility to the common good.[8] The USCCB has consistently voiced the concern for the common good against the dominant American ethos that focuses on individual rights and freedoms. Perhaps the best example of this is their approach to economic justice. Recall that in *Economic Justice for All* the bishops evaluate an economy based on how well it serves the most vulnerable people. The US bishops reiterate

---

7. Pontifical Council for Justice and Peace, "Vocation of the Business Leader: A Reflection" (2014), available at *https://www.stthomas.edu/media/catholicstudies/center/ryan/publications/publicationpdfs/vocationofthebusinessleaderpdf/PontificalCouncil_4.pdf*.

8. John Coleman, "North American Culture's Receptivity to CST," in *Catholic Social Teaching in Global Perspective*, ed. Daniel McDonald (Maryknoll, NY: Orbis, 2010), 198.

themes from *Economic Justice for All* in their statements on globalization. In 1996, for example, they expressed concern about the negative
effect of globalization on the rights of those living in poverty.

> Because the economy has moral dimensions, economic
> choices and institutions must be judged by how they pro-
> tect or undermine the life and dignity of the human person.
> As individuals, all have the right to the basic necessities of
> life—food, education, shelter, medical care, job security, pro-
> ductive work, just wages and working conditions, as well as
> the consequent duty to provide for our families and to con-
> tribute to society. In the globalized economy, these rights
> appear to be much less secure.[9]

Recognizing the connection between the protection of individual
rights and meeting responsibilities to the larger community, the
bishops emphasize the role of solidarity in responding to increasing
global interconnections. This section will explore the work of the
USCCB by examining two pastoral letters, *Called to Global Solidarity* and *A Place at the Table*, and two initiatives, Catholic Relief Services and Catholics Confront Global Poverty campaign, which aim
to promote global solidarity and defend human rights in the context
of globalization.

Called to Global Solidarity

In their 1997 statement *Called to Global Solidarity* (*CGS*), the USCCB
argues that Catholics in the United States have unique responsibilities toward the global common good because they are both members
of a worldwide church and citizens of a nation with influence across
the world. Speaking on behalf of US Catholics, the bishops state, "We
are members of a universal Church that transcends national boundaries and calls us to live in solidarity and justice with the peoples of the
world. We are also citizens of a powerful democracy with enormous
influence beyond our borders" (*CGS*, no. 1).

---

9. USCCB Office of International Justice and Peace, "The Globalized Economy:
Challenges to the Church in the U.S." (1996), available at *http://www.usccb.org/issues
-and-action/human-life-and-dignity/global-issues/trade/presentation-on-globalization
-and-challenges-to-church-in-us-1996-10-05.cfm*.

In the statement, the bishops discuss specific ways that economic globalization has widened the gap between wealthy and impoverished nations. They also note that the globalization of markets, transportation, and communication has increased people's awareness of the interconnectedness of the world. Globalization has also generated greater awareness of the injustices around the world. Specifically, the bishops note that communication technologies and global media allow the world to see images of genocide in Rwanda and Darfur and other cases of crimes against humanity. At the same time, the bishops fear that the awareness of human rights violations has not necessarily led to efforts to eliminate such injustices. Among US citizens, the bishops suggest, "There is increasing complacency about the defense of human rights" (*CGS*, no. 11).

The USCCB insists that apathy toward global injustice contradicts the demands of the Christian faith. National leaders and large agencies are called to respond to injustice, but so are individuals and local communities, the bishops explain. For example, they call on local parishes to integrate a global perspective and commitment to justice into their life and identity. "Catholic communities of faith should measure their prayer, education, and action by how they serve the life, dignity, and rights of the human person at home and abroad" (*CGS*, no. 30). One of the ways that the USCCB has encouraged global responsibility within parishes is through connecting parishes to the Catholic Church's existing international activities. Individual Catholics are often unaware of the charity and justice work of the international Catholic community. Specifically, many Catholics do not know about the work of Catholic Relief Services.

Catholic Relief Services and the Catholics Confront Global Poverty Campaign

Catholic Relief Services (CRS), the USCCB's official international humanitarian agency, is driven by the principles of CST, promoting human dignity, the common good, and solidarity through direct service, education, and advocacy. Since the US bishops established CRS in 1943, the organization has spread throughout the world, now serving more than one hundred million people in more than one hundred countries.[10] CRS's microfinance program provides a good example of the USCCB's work to empower communities living in poverty. By working with community-based savings groups or larger microfinance associations, CRS has provided loans to help low-income groups develop revenue-generating initiatives in their communities. For example, from 2000 to 2008, CRS partnered with local chickpea farmers in Tanzania to organize farmers to create a collaborative Savings and Internal Lending Community (SILC). Within the SILC model, farmers could access loans during peak farming season in order to increase their revenue. With greater revenue, they could invest their profits back into the group savings and benefit the whole group.[11]

In 2005, the USCCB and CRS developed a campaign called "Catholics Confront Global Poverty" to address international poverty by promoting just trade, debt relief, international peace through development, justice for migrants, and effective aid to impoverished countries.[12] The campaign also focuses on environmental justice, seeking to promote the just extraction and distribution of natural resources and combat global climate change. The campaign specifically addresses economic globalization, critiquing liberal trade agreements and agriculture subsidies that exploit poor nations for their natural resources, agricultural products, and labor.

Free Trade vs. Fair Trade

Economic globalization is supported by the opening up of borders to increase the flow of goods and services between nations. This process has been facilitated by free trade agreements such as the 1994 North American Free Trade Agreement between Mexico, Canada, and the United States (NAFTA).

continued

---

10. Catholic Relief Services' website is available at *https://www.crs.org/*.

11. "How Savings-Led Microfinance Has Improved Chickpea Marketing in the Lake Zone of Tanzania" (November 2010), available at *https://www.crs.org/sites/default/files/tools-research/how-savings-led-microfinance-has-improved-chickpea-marketing.pdf*.

12. The history of Catholics Confront Global Poverty is available at *https://www.confrontglobalpoverty.org/learn/about-ccgp/*.

> **Free Trade vs. Fair Trade** *continued*
>
> Free trade agreements such as NAFTA do not necessarily result in equal benefits for all countries. The Carnegie Foundation funded a 2004 study to assess the impact of NAFTA ten years after its implementation. Researchers found that NAFTA had an overall negative impact on the Mexican economy, citing a loss of 1.3 million agriculture jobs and a drop in real wages for the majority of Mexicans since 1994.[13] One of the reasons NAFTA has been particularly hard on the rural population in Mexico, the researchers explain, is that Mexican farmers were unable to compete with large subsidized US farms that were able to sell their products at significantly lower prices.[14] The fair trade movement developed as a way to advocate for farmers in developing countries and inform consumers about the labor practices behind and environmental impact of the products they buy.
>
> The bishops of the United States and Mexico issued a joint statement in response to political debate over the renegotiation of NAFTA in 2017. They urged policy makers to evaluate the trade deal based on its impact on indigenous people and the poor. In the statement, they called for an agreement that promotes sustainable development, protects the rights of workers, and maximizes participation of all people.[15]

The Catholics Confront Global Poverty campaign highlights the effects of globalization on human life and points out how people's decisions can mitigate the harmful effects of globalization. Global poverty and the resulting injustices—hunger, violence, the

---

13. John Audley, Demetrios G. Papademetriou, Sandra Polaski, and Scott Vaughan, "NAFTA's Promise and Reality: Lessons from Mexico for the Hemisphere" (Carnegie Endowment for International Peace, 2004): 6, available at *http://carnegie endowment.org/files/nafta1.pdf.*

14. Ibid., p. 16.

15. United States Conference of Catholic Bishops and Conference of the Mexican Episcopate, "Renegotiating NAFTA: Rebuilding our Economic Relationship in Solidarity, Mutual Trust, and Justice" (November 15, 2017), available at *http:// www.usccb.org/issues-and-action/human-life-and-dignity/global-issues/trade/upload /NAFTA-STATEMENT-ENGLISH.pdf.* For more information about fair trade see *https://www.fairtradecertified.org/* and *https://globalexchange.org/.*

displacement of people, the exploitation of farmers and other workers, environmental degradation, and the sale of vulnerable girls and women to traffickers who promise decent wages and a better life in another country—are not inevitable. The campaign stresses the unrealized influence of the global Catholic community to promote economic justice in the context of globalization. Therefore, it seeks to educate and mobilize one million Catholics to act out of solidarity with the poor and vulnerable.[16] Specifically, the campaign asks Catholics to educate themselves, write to their elected officials on priority issues such as refugee rights, and use social media to raise awareness about human rights.[17]

A Place at the Table

Although the USCCB implores Catholics to take responsibility for the alleviation of poverty, they argue that all people share in this responsibility. In a 2002 pastoral statement, *A Place at the Table* (*PAT*), the US bishops explain how everyone ought to be involved. They argue that "the Catholic way is to recognize the essential role and the complementary responsibilities of families, communities, the market, and government to work together to overcome poverty and advance human dignity" (*PAT*, no. 34). Using the metaphor of a table, the bishops advocate for the alleviation of poverty and wider participation in decision-making. Not only is the table the place where people eat, the bishops point out, the table is also where people gather to make decisions and share the Eucharist. The dynamics of globalization have left many of the world's poor without a place at the table—they lack both sufficient food and a voice in the decisions driving the global economy.

The USCCB suggests that the legs of the table represent entities responsible for preventing and alleviating poverty. The first leg represents individuals and families. The bishops argue against apathy, stating that "every person has a responsibility to respect the dignity of others and to work to secure not only their own rights but also the rights of others" (*PAT*, no. 30). The second leg represents local

---

16. USCCB, Catholics Confront Global Poverty, "The Face of Global Poverty."

17. Catholics Confront Global Poverty website available at *http://www.confront globalpoverty.org/.*

communities, including churches and faith-based organizations. The bishops note that much work is already being done on local levels by faith communities, such as Catholic schools and hospitals, Catholic Charities, and the Catholic Campaign for Human Development. The bishops remind the reader that "faith is a religious commitment; it is also a community resource" (*PAT*, no. 31).

The USCCB calls on businesses and financial institutions that drive the private sector,[18] the table's third leg, to use their influence on the global market to promote justice for the most vulnerable. The bishops advocate for corporate responsibility, stressing the need for collaboration among employers and the labor movement to ensure just wages and decent working conditions. They express particular concern for people living in poverty, arguing, "The process of globalization must provide opportunities for the participation of the poorest people and the economic development of the poorest nations" (*PAT*, no. 32).

Referring to the government as the fourth leg, the US bishops reiterate the Catholic understanding of the positive role government ought to play in protecting the common good. The government, they argue, should "provide a safety net for the vulnerable, and help overcome discrimination and ensure equal opportunity for all" (*PAT*, no. 33). Government regulations are particularly important when communities fail to protect the rights of the most vulnerable (*PAT*, no. 33). The bishops emphasize that all four legs have responsibilities to protect human rights. They call on individuals, faith communities, businesses, and governments to collaborate to overcome challenges to justice that have emerged in the context of globalization.

Reading the Signs of the Times: Globalization and Human Rights

People can ignore the reality of globalization only with great difficulty, and they cannot return to a preglobalized world. Social ethicist Thomas Massaro points out that people cannot reverse the historical process of globalization, but people can and should try to direct it in

---

18. The private sector refers to the part of the economy that is not controlled by the state and tends to be driven by for-profit organizations.

a way that promotes justice. Massaro suggests, "It is no longer a matter of *whether* to globalize, but rather *how* to globalize in a way that protects core values as much as possible."[19] This section will explore some of the debates about the nature and ethical dimensions of globalization. Drawing on the work of Catholic social ethicist David Hollenbach, this section will also highlight the challenge of promoting human rights in an interconnected and diverse world.

The Nature and Impact of Economic Globalization

In 2012 a fire broke out in a garment factory in Dhaka, Bangladesh, killing more than one hundred people, mostly women, many of whom were trapped inside. The tragedy highlighted a widespread problem of unsafe working conditions in the country, the world's second largest exporter of clothing after China. Advocates for worker justice argue that the fire could have been prevented if the factory had taken measures to promote fire safety by providing accessible emergency exits on each floor. In the aftermath of the fire, debates ensued about who bears responsibility to protect such workers. Beyond the obvious responsibility of the factory owners, one can point to US companies such as Walmart that use the factory to supply some of their brands.[20] Advocates for more governmental oversight challenge the United States and Bangladesh for failing to guarantee safe working conditions as a condition for international trade.

One result of globalization has been an increasing interdependence of markets, with greater freedom to move supplies and labor across borders. This context makes it easier for US companies to rely on overseas suppliers. Questions about the nature and ethical implications of economic globalization generate debate. Some for-profit businesses see the potential for global markets to foster development in poor areas and argue that transnational corporations can stimulate the economies of impoverished nations by increasing trade and providing

---

19. Thomas Massaro, *Living Justice: Catholic Social Teaching in Action*, Second Classroom Edition (Lanham, MD: Rowman & Littlefield, 2012), 174.

20. Vikas Bajaj, "Fatal Fire in Bangladesh Highlights the Dangers Facing Garment Workers," *New York Times* (November 25, 2012), available at *http://www .nytimes.com/2012/11/26/world/asia/bangladesh-fire-kills-more-than-100-and-injures -many.html*.

jobs. Critics of globalization, however, note that developing countries tend to lower environmental regulations and labor standards in order to accommodate the wishes of transnational corporations. This argument can be made in the case involving the Bangladesh factory.

The 2016 United Nations World Development Report challenged the assumption that transnational corporations necessarily promote human development. The report points out ways that transnational corporations benefit the wealthy over the poor when corporations situate themselves strategically to avoid taxes or regulations. The UN Development Program argues that globalization can help eradicate poverty, but that this potential can be realized only if governing bodies regulate globalization in new ways. Specifically, the UN Development Program calls for stronger forms of governance to protect developing countries. The 2016 report states,

> Global markets are a great source of dynamism, but they need to be properly regulated to work for the majority. These regulations in turn need to be rooted in legitimate multilateral processes, where the interests of developing countries are central and where the voices of people contribute to the deliberative process. These transformations at the global level are essential for achieving human development for everyone.[21]

With all that has been said about globalization, ethicists have cause for great concern and, at the same time, reasons for hope. For example, a number of transnational nongovernmental organizations have emerged in opposition to sweatshops, advocating for the rights of workers to safe conditions and just wages.[22] Social ethicist David Hollenbach suggests that one of the positive aspects of globalization is that it promotes an awareness of shared humanity, the foundation of human rights. He states,

> The human rights ethos conceives of human beings as, first, members of the worldwide human community with rights that derive from their humanity as such and, second,

21. United Nations Development Program Report (2016), available *at http://hdr .undp.org/sites/default/files/2016_human_development_report.pdf.*

22. Examples include United Students against Sweatshops and Clean Clothes Campaign.

as members of the communities of existing nation states. The globalization of citizenship grants membership in the human community a higher value than citizenship in a particular nation state, at least in extreme situations where humanity itself is threatened.[23]

Hollenbach stresses the need for ongoing dialogue on how to define and promote human rights in a multicultural world. Writing on the context of Africa, Hollenbach suggests that the US notion of human rights is often rejected because it focuses too much on individual freedoms and privacy. One of the problems is that "solidarity with others has little formative role on this individualistic concept of human rights."[24] Hollenbach argues that human rights cannot be construed narrowly as political and civil rights that focus primarily on the protection of individual freedom. To develop a more appropriate and cross-cultural understanding of human rights, individual freedom must be held in relationship to the virtue of solidarity, particularly with the poor. Human rights, especially as seen in developing countries, need to include a strong social dimension, one that touches on people's daily struggles and emphasizes their economic rights.[25]

Hollenbach draws on the Second Vatican Council's approach to human rights to address the modern context. In his reading of *Gaudium et spes*, Hollenbach identifies how rights are framed within the life of a community. The text lists not only basic rights to food and shelter but also to participation in political and economic life—"positive claims to be able to participate actively in the life of the community."[26] Hollenbach makes the point more explicitly: "It was this linkage of the idea of human rights with the common good that enabled the Catholic tradition to see that support for human rights did not require abandonment of the tradition's deep sensitivity to the importance of communal solidarity for human flourishing."[27]

---

23. David Hollenbach, "Life in the Global Community," *America* (November 4, 2002): 7.

24. David Hollenbach, *The Global Face of Public Faith: Politics, Human Rights, and Christian Ethics* (Washington, DC: Georgetown University Press, 2003), 220.

25. Ibid., 228.

26. Hollenbach, "Commentary on *Gaudium et spes*," 281.

27. Ibid.

Summary and Integration for Service Learners

This chapter discussed the Catholic Church's advocacy for the rights and responsibilities of the entire human community, especially in relationship to economic globalization. The Catholic social tradition links human rights with responsibilities, a perspective grounded in a commitment to protect the dignity of the individual and promote the common good. Through writings and campaigns, the USCCB has challenged people to take responsibility for protecting the rights of all, especially of the poor throughout the world.

The principle of rights and responsibilities is particularly relevant as the Catholic Church continues to discern the best responses to globalization, one of the signs of the times that invites theological reflection and ethical responses. The globalization of communication makes it possible for people to learn much about human rights violations around the world and also provides opportunities to overcome national and cultural boundaries to create a dialogue on the meaning of human rights and how to protect them.

Revisit your answers to the questions posed at the beginning of this chapter. Would you answer any of them differently? Do you see globalization more as a threat to human rights or as a way to protect human rights throughout the world? Use the following vignette to reflect further on this topic and to practice the see-judge-act process in relation to it.

See, Judge, Act in the Community

Vignette

For her service-learning experience, Susan decided to partner with a national nonprofit organization to promote fair trade products on college campuses because she wanted to advocate for economic rights on an international scale. During her orientation, she learned about the impact of the fair trade system on coffee farmers in Colombia. When farmers are informed about the real value of their product and empowered to market their product to conscientious consumers, they can receive a just wage and employ more sustainable agricultural practices. Susan found that most people on her campus were willing to pay more for coffee when they learned about the role of fair trade in protecting people's economic rights, and many were surprised that the very small increase in cost for a cup of coffee made a big difference in the living conditions of the coffee growers.

See: Social Analysis

- What does the vignette reveal about economic globalization? How do the college students willing to buy fair trade coffee relate to the process of globalization? How does the Colombian coffee farmer who receives a just wage relate to globalization?
- What conditions—social, political, economic—contribute to the inequalities that the student is addressing by promoting the purchase of fair trade products?

Judge: Ethical Reflection

- How do you understand the relationship between rights and responsibilities in the Catholic social tradition? How would you apply the principle of rights and responsibilities in assessing the situation of Colombian coffee farmworkers who do not receive fair compensation for their work?
- What is the role of Colombian and US governing bodies, nongovernmental organizations, and individuals in protecting people's economic rights? How might the Catholic social principle of solidarity inform your answers?

Act: Promoting Justice

- Consider what you have learned about human rights and responsibilities from CST and the effects of economic globalization. Identify actions or policies that might ameliorate the negative effects of economic globalization by ensuring the protection of human rights throughout the world.
- Select a local organization, perhaps a service-learning setting, that aims to serve the needs of the poor and consider how the organization's efforts relate to economic globalization. Does the organization try to find solutions to problems caused or exacerbated by such globalization? Does the organization take advantage of opportunities made possible because of economic globalization?

Suggestions for Further Social Analysis in a Service-Learning Context

- Read the United Nations *Universal Declaration of Human Rights*. Using the UN declaration as a guide, investigate whether human rights are violated in a service-learning context with which you are familiar.
- Read some perspectives on human rights from different cultural and religious traditions. What are some of the similarities and differences you notice in these perspectives?
- Research the work of multinational nongovernmental organizations that address human rights violations (Amnesty International, Human Rights Watch, etc.). What are some of the issues they address?
- Learn about how some colleges and universities have made the commitment to be fair trade universities at *https://ignatiansolidarity .net/blog/2013/12/04/fair-trade-presentation-fair-trade-universities/*.

For Further Study on Catholic Social Thought on Globalization and Human Rights

Coleman, John, W. F. Ryan, and Bill Ryan. *Globalization and Catholic Social Thought: Present Crisis, Future Hope*. Maryknoll, NY: Orbis Books, 2005.

Finn, Daniel, ed. *The Moral Dynamics of Economic Life: An Extension and Critique of* Caritas in Veritate. New York: Oxford University Press, 2012.

Groody, Daniel. *Globalization, Spirituality, and Justice: Navigating the Path to Peace*. Maryknoll, NY: Orbis Press, 2007.

Hollenbach, David. *The Common Good and Christian Ethics*. Washington, DC: Georgetown University Press, 2002.

———. *The Global Face of Public Faith: Politics, Human Rights, and Christian Ethics*. Washington, DC: Georgetown University Press, 2003.

Appendix

Church Documents Cited

A list of Catholic Church documents cited in the text follows.[1] All Vatican documents can be found at the Vatican's website: *http://w2.vatican.va/content/vatican/en.html.* All US documents can be found at the United States Catholic Conference of Bishops' (USCCB) website: *http://www.usccb.org/.*

Papal, Conciliar, and Synodal Documents

Pope Benedict XVI, *Caritas in veritate (Charity in Truth)*, 2009.

Pope Francis, *Evangelii gaudium (On the Proclamation of the Gospel in Today's World)*, 2013.

Pope Francis, *Gaudete et exsultate (On the Call to Holiness in Today's World)*, 2018.

Pope Francis, *Laudato si': On Care for Our Common Home*, 2015.

Pope John Paul II, *Centesimus annus (On the Hundredth Anniversary of* Rerum Novarum), 1991.

Pope John Paul II, *Evangelium vitae (The Gospel of Life)*, 1981.

Pope John Paul II, *Familiaris consortio (On the Role of the Christian Family in the Modern World)*, 1981.

Pope John Paul II, *Laborem exercens (On Human Work)*, 1995.

Pope John Paul II, *Sollicitudo rei socialis (On Social Concern)*, 1987.

Pope John XXIII, *Mater et magistra (Christianity and Social Progress)*, 1961.

---

1. A note on gender-inclusive language and church documents: This text aims to use gender-inclusive language whenever possible. However, when quoting church documents, it follows the translation offered by the Vatican or USCCB, which may lack such inclusivity.

Pope John XXIII, *Pacem in terris* (*Peace on Earth*), 1963.

Pope Leo XIII, *Rerum novarum* (*On the Condition of Labor*), 1891.

Pope Paul VI, *Octogesima adveniens* (*A Call to Action*), 1971.

Pope Paul VI, *Populorum progressio* (*The Development of Peoples*), 1967.

Pope Pius XI, *Quadragesimo anno* (*The Reconstruction of Social Order*), 1931.

Pope Pius XII, *Exsul familia Nazarethana* (*The Exiled Family from Nazareth*), 1952.

Second Vatican Council, *Ad gentes* (*Decree on the Missionary Activity of the Church*), 1965.

Second Vatican Council, *Dei verbum* (*Dogmatic Constitution on Divine Revelation*), 1965.

Second Vatican Council, *Gaudium et spes* (*Pastoral Constitution on the Church in the Modern World*), 1965.

Synod of Bishops, *Justice in the World*, 1971.

United States Conference of Catholic Bishops Documents

A Fair and Just Workplace: Principles and Practices, 1999.

A Place at the Table, 2002.

Brothers and Sisters to Us: Pastoral Letter on Racism, 1979.

Called to Global Solidarity, 1997.

Economic Justice for All, 1986.

"For I Was Hungry and You Gave Me Food:" Catholic Reflections on Food, Farmers, and Farmworkers, 2003.

Forming Consciences for Faithful Citizenship, published before each presidential election since 1999.

Global Climate Change: A Plea for Dialogue, Prudence, and the Common Good, 2001.

Labor Day Statements, published annually since 1986.

Renewing the Earth: An Invitation to Reflection and Action on Environment in Light of Catholic Social Teaching, 1991.

Sharing Catholic Social Teaching: Challenges and Directions, 1997.

Strangers No Longer: Together on the Journey of Hope. A Pastoral Letter Concerning Migration from the Catholic Bishops of Mexico and the United States, 2003.

The Challenge of Peace: God's Promise and Our Response, 1983.

The Harvest of Justice Is Sown in Peace, 1993.

Index

Note: The abbreviations cap, i, s, or n that follow page numbers indicate captions, illustrations, sidebars, or footnotes, respectively.

SEE, JUDGE, ACT
CATHOLIC SOCIAL TEACHING AND
SERVICE LEARNING, REVISED EDITION

The new edition of *See, Judge, Act* is a splendid introduction to the rich heritage of modern Catholic social teaching. Even more, in the spirit of Pope Francis's pastoral theology, it offers an invaluable guide to *living* the tradition in the context of service learning. Following the hermeneutical logic of the pastoral circle or spiral in responding to the "signs of the times," Brigham brings the wisdom of a vital tradition to bear on a range of critical social issues. *See, Judge, Act* gives us reason to hope that the Church's social teaching will cease to be our "best-kept secret."

—William O'Neill, Jesuit School of
Theology of Santa Clara University

Erin Brigham updates a proven text that delivers the tools needed for reflective community engagement. Designed for readers with little or no theology background, *See, Judge, Act* introduces seven principles of Catholic social teaching and guides students and teachers alike to apply them to contemporary social issues. Using the see-judge-act method of analysis—seeing social situations, judging them in light of CST principles, and acting to promote justice and improve the situations of those served—this resource deftly balances thoughtful reflection with concrete application. With service-learning vignettes, reflection questions that bookend each chapter, rich recommended resources, and sidebars that introduce relevant people, events, and concepts, *See, Judge, Act* invites and empowers students to participate in works of justice an

Erin M. Brigham is
ter for Catholic Stud
theology and social

ANSELM
ACADEMIC
Wir
ww

02 B